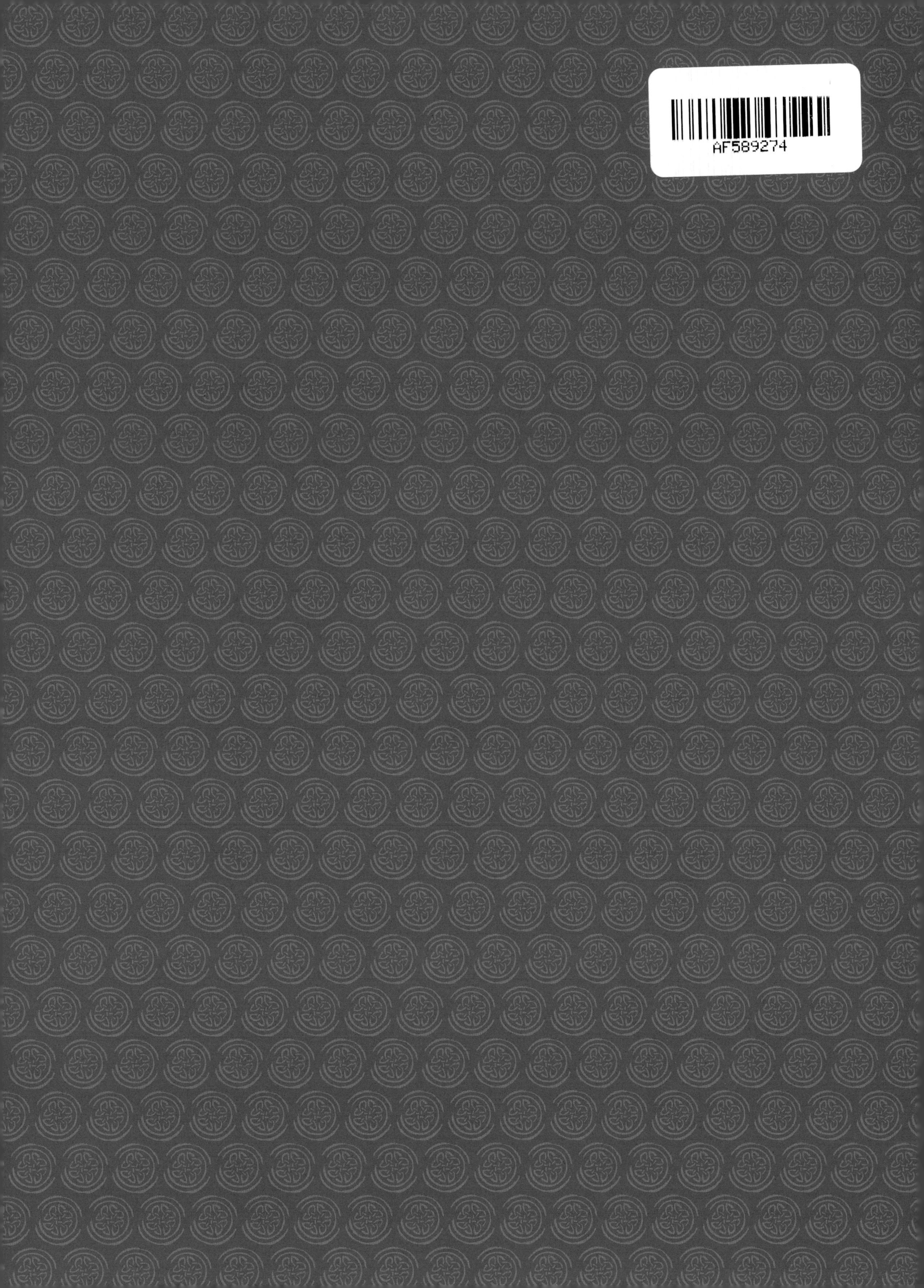

HARE + KLEIN DESIGN

HARE + KLEIN DESIGN

MERYL HARE

PHOTOGRAPHY BY JEN WILDING

CONTENTS

THE DESIGN JOURNEY

I have a rule that I try to adhere to: I would be happy to live in the interiors that we create.

Of course, every home is different. They all start with a unique architectural envelope, they need to suit a range of diverse interests, and they must reflect the owners' personalities. But, that being said, the common thread of our work is our commitment to creating homes that nurture and enrich lives. There is a lot of trust involved in the process of designing the interior of a home. This is something that we are very aware of and that we never take for granted. We have to earn that trust, then use it wisely and responsibly.

So, what are the elements that guide us in creating interiors? Firstly, the clients' way of living and their needs are foremost in our minds. We consider their aesthetic comfort level, which we discuss with them very early in the process. We like to work with them to establish a visual guide. Pictures often speak louder than words, so we explore which of our projects they are drawn to and ask them to share any imagery they have saved from websites, books or social media. It is not that we plan to duplicate any of these interiors, but this process helps to understand their visual taste.

Secondly, we establish the design language that we are aiming to achieve in terms of both design and decoration. We plan the spaces with the furniture that will populate them. Generosity of scale and attention to detail are very important to me, in every project. Then there are the materials and finishes that combine to create colour, texture and contrast. We start with the floors, walls, joinery, lighting and hard surfaces then consider soft furnishings and furniture. It's not an exercise in matching, but rather a juxtaposition of elements to create visual harmony and interest.

One of the most important qualities we strive for in our interiors is comfort – in all its senses. This comes from lighting that is subtle, except where it is required for tasks like reading or cooking or to illuminate artworks, or it may be about the colours and textures in a room, the height of a kitchen benchtop or the physical comfort of the furniture. All these elements combine to create rooms that are a joy to be in.

At the beginning of every project, we dedicate time to establishing a concept that defines what we call the project's 'design language'. This is the spark that ignites and guides our creative process, but there is no particular formula or method for unearthing it. Sometimes it comes in an 'aha' moment, and sometimes it takes longer. There are examples of both kinds of inspiration in this book. For example, in Peppermint Grove the shape of the woodwork on a verandah led to a lightbulb moment that inspired me to design the interleading doors, which established that project's design language. When working on Bridgeview with an overseas client, whom we had never met, it took longer to establish its design language. Regardless of how it emerges, this element of a project is the basic and most important core of the emerging concept.

We assemble finishes – similar to the mood boards opening each chapter of this book – sketch design details, discuss

'THERE IS A LOT OF TRUST INVOLVED IN THE PROCESS OF DESIGNING THE INTERIOR OF A HOME. THIS IS SOMETHING THAT WE ARE VERY AWARE OF AND THAT WE NEVER TAKE FOR GRANTED.'

potential ideas and delve into the unique qualities of the home and the owners' brief until a story begins to emerge. If the kitchen is in a prominent position, we may start our concept there. Alternatively, strong architectural elements might guide our initial thinking.

I love this initial stage of our projects. We present our ideas to our clients, hoping that we have not only interpreted their brief, understood their personalities and responded to their needs, but taken it further than they could have imagined. This is the beginning of a creative journey for all of us. It's a high-five moment!

In many of the homes we design, the kitchen is the focus of family life. It is also a place where guests inevitably linger to chat while their host prepares the meal. As a result, the kitchen is often the most detailed part of our designs, in terms of both function and aesthetics. We have to carefully select materials and finishes that are fit for purpose. Our documentation includes a myriad of technical specifications and details. The kitchen is often an integral element of the design language of a home. In this book, there are several examples of kitchens that fit within the visual tone of the house as a whole. For example, the stone used for an island bench in Skyline Penthouse is repeated as a feature in the living room. The kitchen is also the domain of the people who cook for the family. Our role is to guide the design aesthetic while fulfilling their requirements.

It can sometimes be challenging to find the right furniture pieces or rugs when we are planning the furnishing of a project. Over time we have designed a furniture range that fits with our aesthetic. We have also designed our own rugs, which are handmade in Nepal. Some of these are featured in this book, along with a description of how they were designed and the process from the initial idea to their manufacture.

It will be clear from the homes featured in this book that we don't slavishly follow fads. Obviously, we are aware of trends and innovations in the design world, from new fabrication materials to the shapes of furniture, but they don't all resonate with us. Will it date in two or three years? Is it mainly intended to attract attention on social media? Interior design trends come and go with bewildering speed, almost as quickly as fast fashion. A new look that is garnering media attention is not necessarily good design. I know we have succeeded when a home we have designed looks even better years later, after it's settled in, the landscaping has matured, and the owners have added their own objects and art with confidence.

I hope this book provides you with inspiration, practical ideas and the confidence to uncover a design language for your own home. I wish for you the same thing that I hope for myself in all our projects: that you are happy to live in the interior that you create.

WOLF
WOLF

INTERIOR DESIGN: CRISTINA REPETI
INTERIOR DECORATION: MADDIE HELYER
LANDSCAPE DESIGN: STUDIO U.C
BUILDER: STRATTI BUILDING

WOOLLAHRA TERRACE

This carefully constructed interior honours the histories of the house and the owners

'THERE IS A RESPECTFUL DIALOGUE BETWEEN THE ORIGINAL TERRACE AT THE FRONT AND THE MORE CONTEMPORARY EXTENSION AT THE REAR.'

Over many years, I have had the privilege of working with the owners of this Victorian terrace. It is situated in a leafy street in the Sydney suburb of Woollahra, which means 'lookout' in the language of the Gadigal people of the Eora Nation, who are the original inhabitants and traditional custodians of this land.

From their first house – bought when their first child was born – to a larger home when the family expanded, a beach house, an interim home and now the downsizer, it's been a journey that I think we have all enjoyed.

They asked me to look at Woollahra Terrace before they made the decision to purchase it, and I expressed my concern that, as it was much smaller than their previous homes, they would have to do some serious culling. They embraced the challenge, but not in the way any of us envisaged. During construction they placed almost all their furniture, art and personal possessions in storage and went on an extended overseas holiday. While they were away, the storage facility burnt to the ground. With the exception of three steel side tables, they lost everything. It was a devastating loss – furniture can be replaced but sentimental items and art can't.

When they purchased it, the terrace was tired. It needed renovating and changes to suit the owners' requirements. It's such an advantage knowing your clients' taste and way of life. The mutual trust we had established over the years made the task of re-creating this home to meet their expectations a little easier. They also have a deep interest and understanding of both the design process and furniture design and were open to new ideas.

We embraced the original features of the front living and dining rooms, retaining the timber floorboards, skirtings, cornices and joinery, but replacing the fireplaces. Staining the floors, installing new pendant lights, painting the joinery on either side of the fireplaces in a dark charcoal and painting the walls in soft tones that complement the living room wallcoverings allowed the rooms to retain their origins while giving them an eclectic update. Some of the new furnishings and art hark back to the owners' previous collection, such as the mirror over the dining fireplace – the original was antique black with similar patterning. It gives them a sense of continuity.

The north-facing, more contemporary living area is the hub of the home. A new functional kitchen supports an eat-in dining table and a small sitting area that faces a new fireplace. The pièce de résistance is the iconic Papa Bear chair placed in front of the courtyard, which is visible from the entrance. We call it the heirloom chair, as it will be handed down through generations of this family. There is also a tiny guest cloakroom under the stairs that is surprisingly glamorous.

The upper level was reconfigured to create two studies, two bathrooms, a laundry and the main bedroom. The lack of space is compensated for by thoughtful and efficient customised storage and furnishings, making the rooms fit for purpose and reflecting the owners' personalities.

This is a highly resolved and carefully constructed interior with a timeless palette that honours the histories of the home and its owners. There is a respectful dialogue between the original terrace at the front and the more contemporary extension at the rear. The teamwork between the owners, the builders, the landscapers and our team contributed to the creation of a lovely new home for a special family, who have graciously accepted their loss and embraced their future.

PREVIOUS: The contemporary Moooi pendant gives off a soft indirect light in the original living room – marrying tradition with modernity.

ABOVE: We replaced the fireplace surround with a pared-back version of the original and painted the existing joinery on either side in Porter's Paints 'Caraway'.

OPPOSITE: The mirror over the mantel is a reminder of the antique Victorian mirror the owners lost in the fire.

NORBERT WOLF
ART DECO
Russell Drysdale
Waves of Living
EARTH & FIRE
ARRANGING THINGS
Artists at Home
Karina Dias Pires
RADICAL CLAY
HISTORY YEAR BY YEAR
JEFFREY SMART
BEN QUILTY
1001 Movie Posters

Twenty Homes One Kitchen
BEAUTIFUL AUSTRALIAN HOMES VOLUME II
IN TOUCH KELLY HOPPEN
Tom Kundig Houses 2
INTERIORS
DREAMING THE LAND
TIM FLACH DOGS

OPPOSITE: This painting has special significance as the owners bought it in Paris, when we were on a buying trip together. Fortunately it wasn't in storage at the time of the fire.

ABOVE: The Papa Bear chair, designed by Hans Wegner in 1951 and made by PP Møbler, is the archetype for a comfortable easy chair and an investment for life.

PREVIOUS: The new kitchen maximises the space available, with detailed bespoke joinery and an attached casual dining table, and connects the transitional internal courtyard and the back terrace.

ABOVE LEFT: Detail of the layered entry console with a Joe Furlonger painting above.

ABOVE RIGHT: The family room sofa is anchored by a silk rug from Tibet Galleries and flanked by one of three side tables that were saved and restored after the fire.

ABOVE: The distinctive Literatura bookcase in the study is a contemporary classic that adds an intriguing third dimension and houses a collection of small treasures.

MINT

OPPOSITE: The grass-cloth wallcovering gives an illusion of space and texture in the compact main bedroom.

ABOVE: A painting by Susie Dureau over the mantel adds calm and depth, reflecting the soft hues of the furnishings.

RIGHT: A cosy window seat faces out to the balcony and the tree-lined street below.

ABOVE: The vanity, fabricated from Silver Adana marble with tapware finished in aged iron, is a pared-back solution to a small bathroom.

OPPOSITE: The guest cloakroom is tucked under the stairs and makes up for its small size with a touch of glamour.

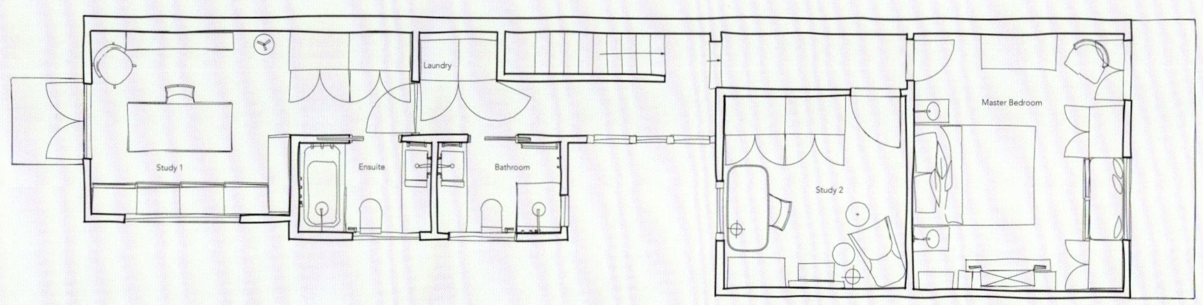

LEFT: Natural light gently highlights a painting by David Pearce.

OPPOSITE: We redesigned the narrow staircase, removing the original balustrade and replacing it with a finer steel one. The internal courtyard on the right brings light and ventilation into the centre of the house.

INTERIOR DESIGN: KRISTIE NIXON
INTERIOR DECORATION: MADDIE HELYER
BUILDER: EASTERN BUILT
ADDITIONAL PHOTOGRAPHY: SEBASTIAN MRUGALSKI

THE WAREHOUSE

A reimagined factory takes working from home
to a whole new level

'LIGHTING WAS CAREFULLY DESIGNED SO THAT THE LIGHT THROUGHOUT IS FILTERED, OBSCURE AND INDIRECT.'

This semi-industrial property in Sydney was built in 1915, after a fire that destroyed the original building on the site. Over the past century, it has been used as a tobacco works, a bulk hardware store, a sheet metal manufactory and a clothing factory. It is a typical, modest example of an early 20th-century three-storey commercial/industrial building, with simplified exterior detailing. The most notable feature is the triangular shape that follows the boundaries of the allotment.

We were at the beginning of the pandemic when planning and construction started. The interior was in a state of disrepair, so there was initial work to be done to make the site safe. Our client originally wanted to create an office space that felt like home, and a home that incorporated an office. The brief expanded to include a gym, a wellness area, and a cosy wine cellar that would double as a bar.

The owner stressed from the beginning of the project that indirect lighting was a requirement throughout the property. Indirect lighting is a feature that Hare + Klein aspire to incorporate in our projects, so we designed the lighting with this in mind. Lighting was carefully designed so that the light throughout is filtered, obscure and indirect. Most of the general lighting is within custom-designed ceiling lighting slots that house reflective LED strips.

The top level is equipped with a full kitchen, with a butler's pantry, and a laundry. There are also casual living and dining areas, plus a small, private work area tucked into the corner. The main bedroom ensuite has a gorgeous circular shower with a skylight that brings in shards of light. There is provision on this level for a circular staircase that will lead up to a roof garden and a small pool.

The first level incorporates the office and includes a comfortable break-out lounge area and a boardroom space. The boardroom is delineated by original blackbutt rafters and two oversized pendants – each 1.3 metres in diameter – over the table. We introduced curves into this floorplan to soften the angular lines and create an intriguing space in the ensuite, as well as reflecting the design language of the floor above.

We designed the small spa facility to incorporate a steam room, shower, toilet, sauna and an ice tub – all within approximately 12 square metres! It's an efficient use of highly detailed space, and it works.

The burnished black-oxide concrete floor with aggregate showing through was the foundation of the palette of dark materials that we adopted throughout. Other materials include walls finished in dark hand-waxed stucco, joinery finished in dark veneers and laminates, slabs of quartzite stone, and hot-rolled steel applied as wall cladding. There are punctuations of walnut, bronze mirror, recycled blackbutt salvaged from the building and even touches of antique brass.

Together, these elements soften an otherwise stark interior and create a sophisticated backdrop for furnishings that were selected with comfort in mind. This former industrial building has been successfully transformed into a home that is both surprising and unexpectedly inviting.

PREVIOUS: The original rough industrial staircase is transformed with a seemingly simple steel balustrade, hand-applied set plaster to the walls, and timber treads and risers.

OPPOSITE: The glass-walled lift exposes the original bricks and is flanked by two vertical indirect lights. A timber step, made from the building's old beams, leads to the bedroom.

ABOVE: The lighting on the staircase is subtle, both day and night.

ABOVE: A steel-and-glass pivot door leads from the stairwell to the first-level entry.

OPPOSITE: Exposed original timber beams, columns and rafters define the boardroom area.

A MAN & HIS WATCH
RAMESH
WATCHES
Thom Browne.
Atlas of Never Built Architecture
MAPPLETHORP

WAREHOUSE HOME
10

PREVIOUS: A comfortable custom-designed modular sofa upholstered in linen forms a cosy area for watching television.

OPPOSITE: The building's industrial past is reflected in the tough finishes applied in the kitchen joinery as well as the concrete floor with aggregate showing through.

ABOVE: Custom-designed ceiling slots house LED strips that are angled to indirectly reflect the light.

RIGHT: The island bench features dramatic Metaurus granite, introducing pattern and texture into the space.

ABOVE: A detail of the drink-preparation niche, surrounded by Eveneer Ravenna veneer joinery.

OPPOSITE: The wine cellar's bar columns are constructed from recycled blackbutt beams, and the tasting table is topped with Port Laurent marble.

OPPOSITE: Hand-waxed stucco finishes the walls in the bedroom, which also features an overlay of soft materials and inbuilt lighting.

ABOVE: A glimpse of the guest cloakroom, concealed behind a pivot joinery door and lined with a reconstituted veneer.

OPPOSITE: The softly lit, cedar-lined sauna is part of the 12-square-metre spa.

ABOVE LEFT: The ice bath is tucked into a curved wall within the small spa area.

ABOVE RIGHT: The steam room is finished in glass mosaics, including the curved bench. An open shower connects the steam room to the sauna.

ABOVE LEFT: The ensuite vanity is made from Portoro quartzite and has a custom steel-framed mirror above.

ABOVE RIGHT: Detail of the guest cloakroom, lined in reconstituted veneer, with a countertop basin in Nero Marquina marble.

ABOVE LEFT: The shape of the shower reflects the curved outer wall and is finished in microcement.

ABOVE RIGHT: The small bathroom in the spa features a freestanding basin in Nero Marquina marble and a ceiling-mounted Inciso spout.

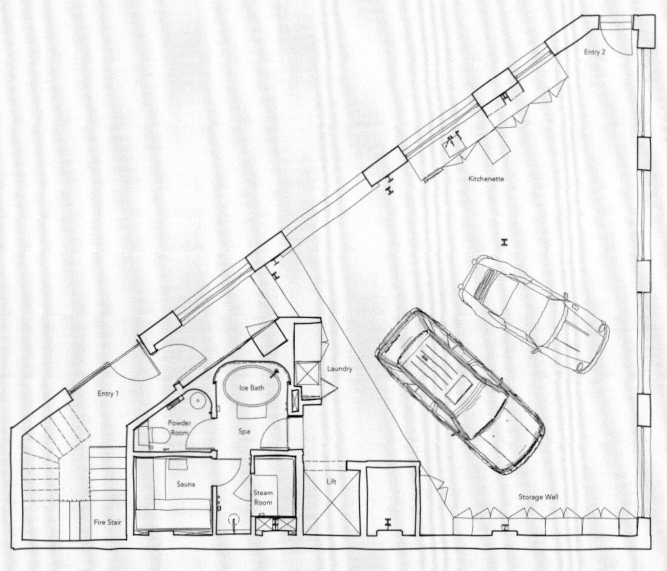

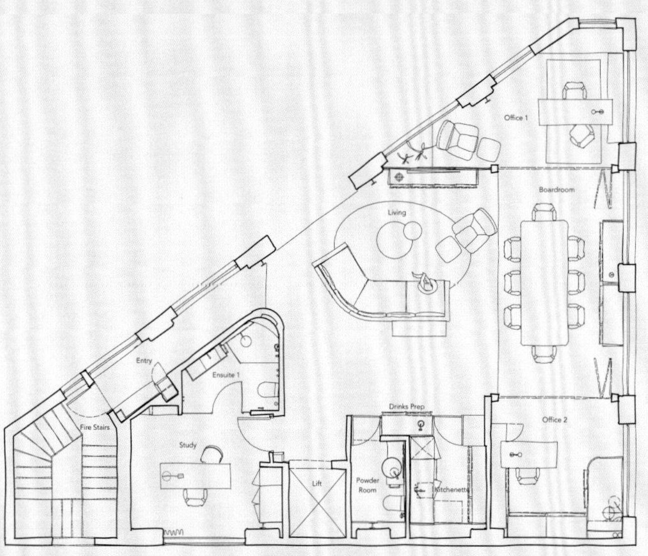

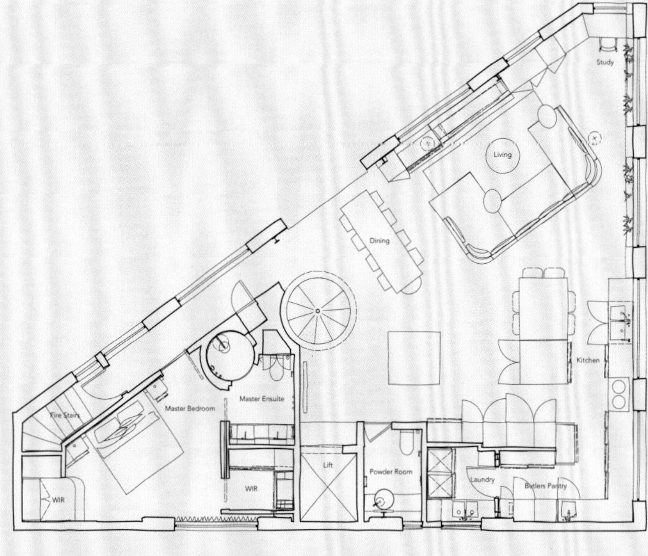

OPPOSITE: The original roller door on the second level was previously used for hoisting materials. We created a metal planter that serves as a balustrade.

A MAN & HIS WATCH
RAMESH
WATCHES
Atlas of

INTERIOR DECORATION: MERYL HARE

THE CHATEAU

The infusion of dramatic contemporary decor
to a century-old French-style home

'BY EMBRACING ITS ORIGINAL STYLE AND HONOURING ITS HISTORY, THIS CONTEMPORARY HOME IS AT EASE IN ITS ANTIPODEAN SETTING.'

It may seem strange that a chateau with strong French architectural detailing exists in South Australia. It was built in 1920 by a dedicated Francophile and, although it has been extended over the past 100 years, the original structure is intact and has acquired a delightful patina over the last century. Also remaining is much of the architectural detailing, including a grand central staircase off the entry. The house sits comfortably in a traditional French-style garden, where established trees and water features are the backdrop for antique and contemporary sculptures.

This was our second collaboration with the owners. We had worked on their former home a few years ago, so mutual trust was already established. As avid collectors of Australian contemporary art and objects, they were drawn to the generous proportions of this house. Their brief asked us to integrate their art collection and to include furniture from their former home, while responding to the scale and architecture of the original building. They also wanted interiors that were elegant and sophisticated, but felt comfortable and relaxed.

Our most important responsibility was to create warm, inviting, and purposeful rooms – otherwise, they could fall into disuse and become cold and unwelcoming. The grand and dramatic scale of many of the rooms – some with 3.8-metre ceilings! – presented an opportunity to work on a generous scale, in terms of both art and furniture, but we were careful to keep our core purpose in mind.

One of my favourite rooms is the study, located just off the entry. It faces south and has bay windows that look out to the front garden. It is cool in summer but the fireplaces on both sides transform it into a cosy retreat in winter. The rich plum velvet sofas bring warmth to the space, and the iconic mid-century pendant over the seating creates a wonderful play on light that emphasises the art and the textured natural weave of the wallcoverings. It is a delightful room to relax and work in.

The curved steel-and-glass French doors that face to the north and the south dominate the summer living room, and a high skylight illuminates it even more. We gave this open-plan room a human scale by creating zones within zones. The living area is defined by a large rug, woven in Nepal, that acts as both a visual platform for the substantial sofas and a subtle room divider. The dining area is emphasised by the modernist chandelier over the dining table, which sits on a textured silk rug. The play of textures – handwoven rugs, the plaited leather ottoman, the glass side table, velvet stools, the timber and lush fabrics – give this room its warmth and character.

The main suite is a joy! The hero piece of this room is *Supreme*, Fiona McMonagle's painting of Diana Ross. It inspired our approach and the palette of deep azure and golden highlights. In such a large space – with ceilings that are 3.3 metres high – the four-poster bed with its layers of luxurious coverings creates a sense of sanctuary. Again, the textured wallcovering brings a calming sense of enclosure.

The innovative aspects of the design of this project lie in the infusion of dramatic, contemporary interior decor to an existing French vernacular. By embracing its original style and honouring its history, this contemporary home is at ease in its antipodean setting. The delightfully confident and eclectic art collection of the owners, and their enthusiasm, understanding and participation in the process, made this a truly collaborative project.

PREVIOUS: The view from the entrance across the porte cochère to the front gate is an unchanged feature of the original house.

OPPOSITE: The view looking back to the entry reveals the decorative iron balustrade that curves around the staircases and the original herringbone timber floors, which have been refinished in a walnut stain.

ABOVE: A collection of vases by Karlien van Rooyen and Kerryn Levy sits in front of a Guido Maestri painting that brings colour and energy into the room.

PREVIOUS: The view from the double entry doors takes in Ben Quilty's *Head of the Table,* a sculpture by Guido Maestri sitting on a round table designed by Patricia Urquiola, and the double staircase.

OPPOSITE: The dramatically scaled, open-plan living, dining and kitchen space is given human scale, with the seating area defined by a Tibet Gallery rug and an oversized Minotti sofa. The recessed windows are left bare, with sheer curtains softening the centre.

ABOVE: The modernist Atelier de Troupe chandelier was placed against the original arched windows as a contrast of styles, while also being reflective of the shapes of the room.

ABOVE LEFT: One of Cassie Thring's delightfully quirky sculptures stands in front of a painting by Ghostpatrol.

ABOVE RIGHT: A classic Gio Ponti armchair creates a reading corner, and a Mito standing lamp, designed by Tom Fereday, and a rug from our second collection are perfect additions.

OPPOSITE: The media room is furnished with much of the owners' prior collection, with the addition of a pair of high-backed, sculptural Longwave armchairs in aqua velvet.

KINFOLK
THE LITTLE BLACK JACKET
marcel wanders

brett whiteley drawings
Alexander McQueen Unseen

MANET
CASSATT
KANDINSKY
DALI
DEGAS
IBIZA
Resident Dog
Vivid
Axel Vervoordt
Portraits of Interiors

PREVIOUS: The winter lounge, which doubles as a study, is flanked by two rich-burgundy sofas and a pair of Platner armchairs in front of the fireplace. Two sculptures – a Paul Sloan figurine on the coffee table and Vipoo Srivilasa's piece on the sofa console – add to the room's delightful ambience.

OPPOSITE: A pleated silk-and-hemp rug sits beneath the antique desk. A pendant light shaped as an open book adds to the layers of colour, texture and art.

ABOVE: A Tom Dixon Wingback chair sits in front of the dramatic Juz Kitson wall sculpture.

PREVIOUS AND OVERLEAF: The generous proportions of the main bedroom embrace a four-poster bed, desk and chaise, overlooked by Fiona McMonagle's portrait of Diana Ross. Cotton sheers, along with textures of grass cloth, velvet, linen, felted wool and silk, create a calm and luxurious sanctuary.

ABOVE: The dressing room embellishments reflect the crystal chandelier of the adjacent ensuite.

OPPOSITE: The antique French chandelier is juxtaposed with the contemporary Shuffle side table and the freestanding bath.

OPPOSITE: The original facade of the chateau, looking through the arched windows to the courtyard. Antique French urns and topiary are in keeping with the traditional French-style landscaping.

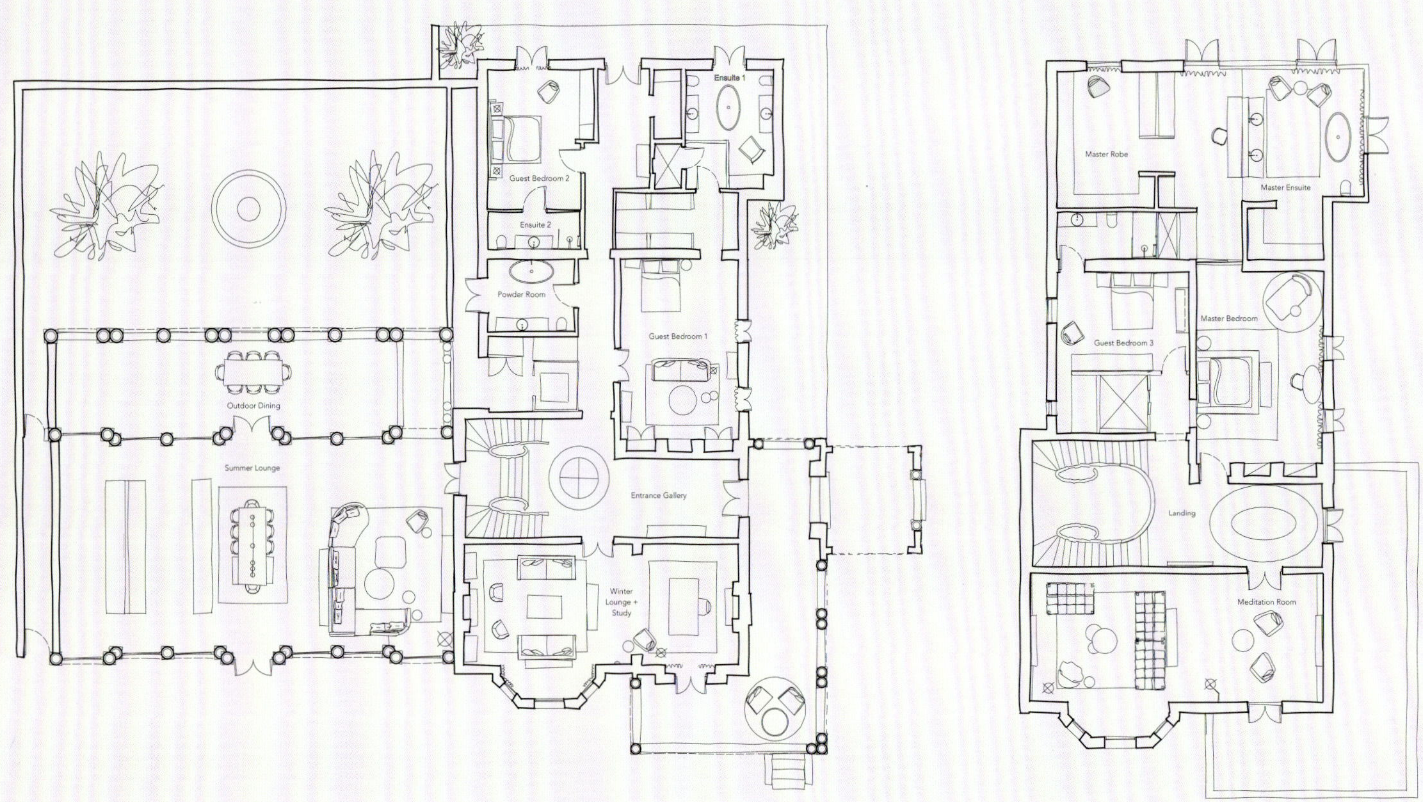

DESIGN INSIGHT: LANDSCAPE

A Nepalese hand-knotted rug inspired by Sydney Harbour at sunset

Our hand-knotted rugs are a collaboration with the Australian company Designer Rugs. We design them and they are made in Kathmandu, Nepal. It is a long process, from the original sketch to the selection of materials, the type of weave and the translation of the design to a digital interpretation that is ultimately followed by the master weavers in Nepal. Although referred to as being woven, the rugs are actually hand-knotted – a process that makes them extremely robust. They are made from Tibetan highland sheep's wool, hemp and silk – all hand spun and dyed and then knotted on looms by skilled weavers. The inconsistency of the fibre thickness and the nature of the hand-dyeing methods inevitably result in colour variations. This process is called abrash, and it ensures that each rug is slightly different and therefore unique.

I went to Nepal to gain an understanding of the production process. Not only was it truly awe-inspiring, but I now appreciate the time it takes to make these rugs, as every process is done by hand. Tibetan rug making has a history that goes back for centuries, and these skills were brought to Nepal in the 1950s by refugees.

The design of this rug, Landscape, was inspired by the view at sunset from my home on Middle Harbour in Sydney, with moody clouds and the water glistening and reflecting the sky above. In this setting, the colours complement the corner of the main bedroom and anchor the chaise in this glorious space.

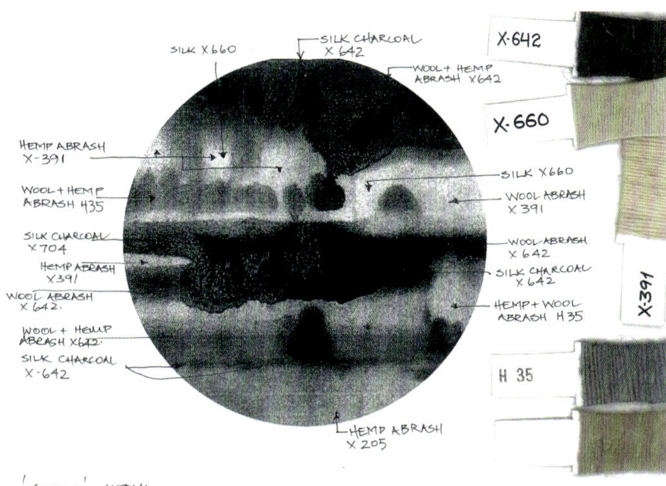

DESIGNER: MERYL HARE
MANUFACTURED BY: DESIGNER RUGS AUSTRALIA
MANUFACTURING METHOD: HAND KNOTTING
MATERIALS: TIBETAN WOOL, HEMP, SILK

INTERIOR DESIGN: CRISTINA REPETI
INTERIOR DECORATION: MERYL HARE
LANDSCAPE DESIGN: SPIRIT LEVEL
BUILDER: STRATTI BUILDING

THE BEACH

A beach house defined by its setting,
from bush to beach

Brodware
AUSTRALIAN MADE SINCE 1964

'IT'S A "KICK OFF YOUR SHOES AT THE FRONT DOOR" TYPE OF HOUSE.'

Perched on the edge of the beach on the western shoreline of Broken Bay in the Central Coast region of New South Wales, this north-east-facing house begins each day drenched in morning sunlight. As the owners said on our first visit, 'Our house is a transition – from the bush as you enter to the beach in front.'

It's what defines the home. On approach, the bush is unspoilt, with indigenous trees and shrubs in nurturing shades of green and grey. On the other side is a pristine beach. It's a perfect combination for a relaxed lifestyle.

We have worked with this client over many years, and have forged a lovely trusting friendship. After downsizing to a smaller city home, they planned to use this beach house for holidays and long weekends. However, they love spending time here and it has become much more than that. It's a 'kick off your shoes at the front door' type of house, which accommodates their family, friends and Molly, their much-loved dog.

Taking our cue from the 'bush to beach' setting, it made sense to start the journey at the entry, using tones that are sympathetic to the bush. In this part of the home, the bedrooms, entry and media room are darker, cooler and more intimate, creating a sanctuary effect. The spaces on the other side of the house are brighter, acknowledging the coastal outlook with accents of deeper colours that reflect the sand, kelp, sea and rocks.

We redesigned the kitchen, introducing an island bench in black metal and stainless steel as a foil to the clean white cabinets and terrazzo bench. The new island bench became the anchor to the living, dining and kitchen area, and is balanced by the black steel fireplace positioned opposite it on a concrete bench, which also serves as extra seating in the living room.

Our challenge was to incorporate and curate those items of furniture and art from their original home that we considered appropriate with this more contemporary Scandinavian aesthetic. They wanted to create a home that embraced their future, but also reflected their past. This layering of contemporary elements in both the design and decor, using a mix of art and objects they have collected over the years, has visually warmed the home and made it personal and welcoming yet low maintenance – perfect for a beach house.

This eclectic, interesting interior surprises and delights the eye. It has quirky elements – such as the Ardmore monkey cushions in the TV room, paired with the BD Barcelona Design Monkey table – but the overall feel is warm, uncluttered and homely, reflecting the owners' personalities and taste.

For us, the real joy of this project is the outcome for our clients. This house was completed a few years ago and has stood the test of time. It offers a calm respite from their busy city lives, and is much loved by the family – including Molly – and their friends.

PREVIOUS: Molly, the beloved golden retriever, lies comfortably on the Turkish kilim next to an iconic Flag Halyard reclining chair by Hans Wegner and a Gear floor lamp, in front of a Jenny Sages artwork.

OPPOSITE: A line of sight from the bush to the beach, with a rug running the length of the corridor from the central courtyard to the media room.

ABOVE: The 'bush' entry is characterised by darker shades and features a welcoming Gervasoni rocking chair and an entry console with a moody Martin King artwork above and baskets for shoes below.

ABOVE: The view to the central courtyard takes in a casual Trim dining table with Carl Hansen Sawback chairs, designed by Hans Wegner, and Caravaggio pendants above.

OPPOSITE: The hero of the kitchen is the Vipp island bench, above which we hung a suspended Troag pendant.

ARE + KLEIN INTERIOR
moments

PREVIOUS: With artworks by Jenny Sages (left) and Emily Kame Kngwarreye (right), the living area is subtly visually separated from the kitchen behind, with the fireplace as a visual foil.

OPPOSITE: An open-plan study on the landing at the top of the stairs is a quiet corner, with watercolours by Joan Macy.

ABOVE: Another iconic piece by Hans Wegner, the Circle chair, has a simple and elegant shape and is hand-finished by PP Møbler.

OPPOSITE: We painted the walls in a blue-black shade, in keeping with the darker side of the home. A playful Monkey side table by Jaime Hayon talks to the monkey cushion fabric by Ardmore.

ABOVE: Coffee table objects include a beautiful bowl by Ruth Levine, constructed using upcycled materials.

OPPOSITE: The main bedroom features bluish grey – the owners' favourite colour.

ABOVE LEFT: Detail of a typical bathroom, simple in concept.

ABOVE RIGHT: A bedroom on the bush side of the home.

OVERLEAF: Views from the terrace to the beach and the headland from the back of the house. We furnished the terrace with a deep and comfortable outdoor sofa, chairs and chaises, creating a perfect place to relax.

Beach Deck
Living
Centre Deck
Media Room
Stairs
Ensuite
Bedroom 2
Entry
Enclosed Entry
Rear Deck
Kitchen
Laundry
Powder Room
Master Bedroom
Master Ensuite
Stairs
Bath
Bedroom 3
Study
Bedroom 4

ORGETTABLE DRESSES HAL RUBENSTEIN
ALIA IN STYLE
SHAPED THE MODERN WORLD Alan J Whiticker

DESIGN INSIGHT: THE NASH

A versatile piece designed for function and aesthetics

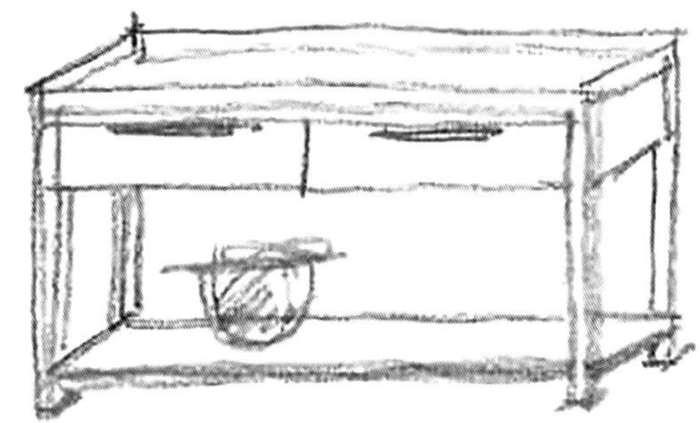

I used to wonder how furniture and fabric names were chosen. Now, as a proud grandmother of four, I have the answer – at least in my case! The Nash is named for my eldest grandson. It is a robust, useful and good-looking piece of furniture – just like its namesake.

Like many of our furniture designs, the Nash evolved as a useful piece. In this case, as a console with two drawers and a shelf for books, baskets or whatever. The ability to have it made in various timber colours, as well as colour options for the metal tray and leather handles, makes it versatile. It works in different interiors, from casual to formal and everything in-between. We have placed it in entry ways, bedrooms, and living and dining rooms.

The original sketch for the Nash is pretty much how it is made, except that we changed the original steel trays to powder-coated aluminium to make it lighter and prevent rusting. The custom handles come in different colours of leather and there is a choice of metal ends – from plain black to bronze, brass or silver. These small details make it special, just like adding a piece of jewellery to an outfit.

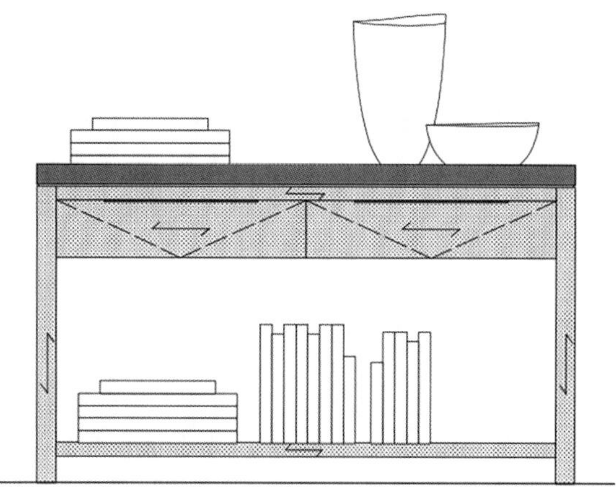

DESIGNER: HARE + KLEIN STUDIO

MANUFACTURED: SYDNEY

MATERIALS: AMERICAN OAK, POWDER-COATED ALUMINIUM, LEATHER, BRASS DETAIL

INTERIOR DESIGN: KRISTIE NIXON
INTERIOR DECORATION: MADDIE HELYER
ARCHITECTURE: JAMES DESIGN STUDIO
LANDSCAPE DESIGN: SECRET GARDEN
BUILDER: SANDLIK

TAYLORS BAY

A house of mixed architectural styles is reimagined as a contemporary light-filled home with subtle reference to its late-Federation origins

'SMALL SPATIAL CHANGES THROUGHOUT THE INTERIOR HAVE DRAMATICALLY ENHANCED THE LIVEABILITY OF THIS FAMILY HOME.'

This is a story of an ugly duckling that was transformed into a beautiful swan. In the beginning, this house was built in the late-Federation style, but over the years it underwent several inappropriate renovations and additions, including some faux French Provincial adornments. It became a confusing mix of architectural styles and had an unattractive street facade.

The owners, an unpretentious family with four teenage children, purchased the house because of its great position – it sits on a large, flat block overlooking Taylors Bay, a small intimate sandy cove on Sydney Harbour. The interior was a bit of a rabbit warren of disconnected and dark unused rooms – they were uninviting spaces that needed purpose and more natural light. In typical Federation style, the ground level had a long dark corridor running down the centre. Unfortunately, the original staircase had been replaced by a French Provincial-style balustrade, which added to the confusion of architectural styles. It became evident early on that structural changes were needed to achieve the home's full potential. As the extent of the external works increased, we introduced the owners to the architects.

The architects redesigned both the front and back facades, introducing light into dark areas by linking the south-facing front to the north-facing back garden. They referenced the home's original late-Federation style with subtle detailing, particularly on the street facade. As the back of the house faces north, it is flooded with sunlight. The deck was extended to connect the main living area with the newly landscaped garden and pool, and adjustable blades control the light and weather. The deck is now protected from the elements and serves as an outdoor room.

Unused rooms were redesigned, opened up and given a new purpose. What was once a dark dining room is now linked with steel-and-glass doors on the living room side and repurposed as a craft and sewing space. It is also connected with the original formal front room, which we redesigned as a cosy informal library. Small spatial changes throughout the interior have dramatically enhanced the liveability of this family home.

I love visiting this home. It has a light and easy aesthetic, it's comfortably elegant and casual, with space for everyone to work, play and retreat to, and it suits the owners' busy lifestyles and the demands of their high-energy teenagers.

PAGE 98: On the right side of the passage, we lined the walls with veneer, creating a light-coloured timber 'box' that holds the guest cloakroom and spare bedroom. The steel-and-glass doors lead to the living area and terrace.

PREVIOUS: To create the dining area, we aligned the stone floor with the raised section of the roof that includes high north-facing windows for light and ventilation.

OPPOSITE: We designed a curved sofa that faces both the fire and the television, but still invites conversation.

ABOVE: The new terrace creates a generous extension to the living room and connects it to the garden and pool.

RIGHT: This delightful focal point in the garden is well used by the family.

ABOVE: Light floods through the skylight above into the stairwell and bounces off the hand-waxed stucco finish on its wall.

OPPOSITE: The Beryl Miles painting brings colour to the upstairs hallway.

INTERIOR DESIGN REVIEW
DEAN PHILLIPS
SECRET GARDENS
LANDSCAPE
FROM THE EARTH
SUPERHOUSE
ACCESSORIES
VILLAS
Kerry Hill

OPPOSITE: The study is on the south side, with a new balcony, designed by the architects, giving it a spacious feel.

ABOVE: The guest cloakroom on the ground level doubles as a guest ensuite.

OPPOSITE: Sliding steel-and-glass doors connect the living room to a small sewing room and, beyond that, the reading room with its Moooi Meshmatics chandelier.

ABOVE: The reading room off the entry has become a favourite quiet space for the family to retreat to, especially to sit in front of the fire in winter.

ABOVE: The design of the vanity in the main ensuite reflects the visual language throughout the home. The layout was reconfigured by raising the bath to allow bathers to enjoy the garden view.

OPPOSITE: The deep charcoal-blue wallcovering in the main bedroom is complemented by a custom headboard with integrated lighting, and sumptuous fabrics.

Aesop.
Aesop.

OPPOSITE: The basement bathroom, next to the gym, is finished with strong, earthy finishes, reflecting the rumpus room behind.

ABOVE: The rumpus room also serves as a media room. It has been given a warm, playful feel with Ardmore wallpaper with a menagerie of cavorting African animals, and a painting by Joanna Kitas.

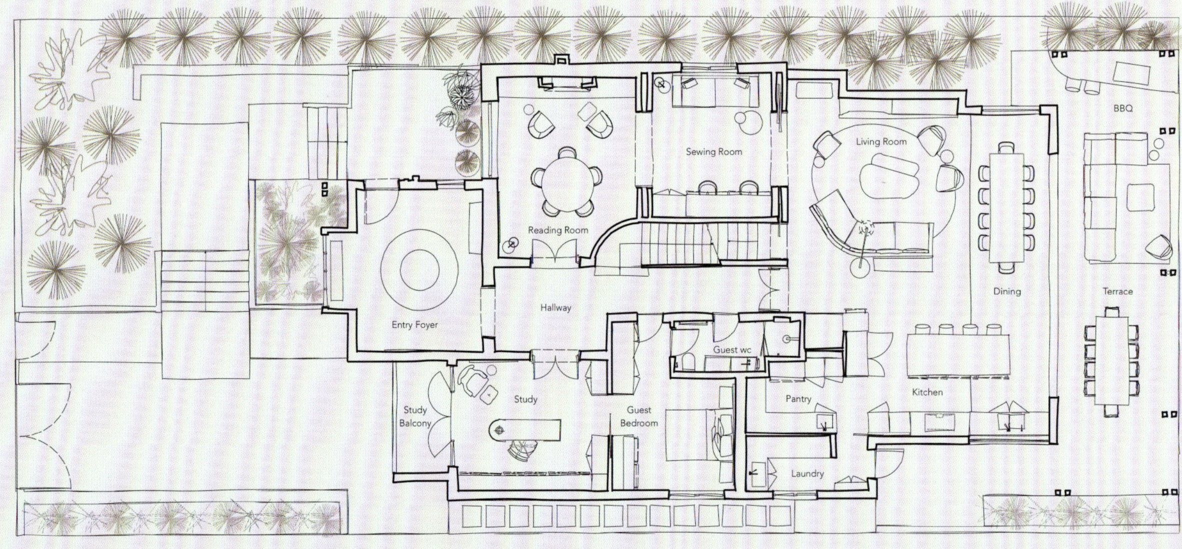

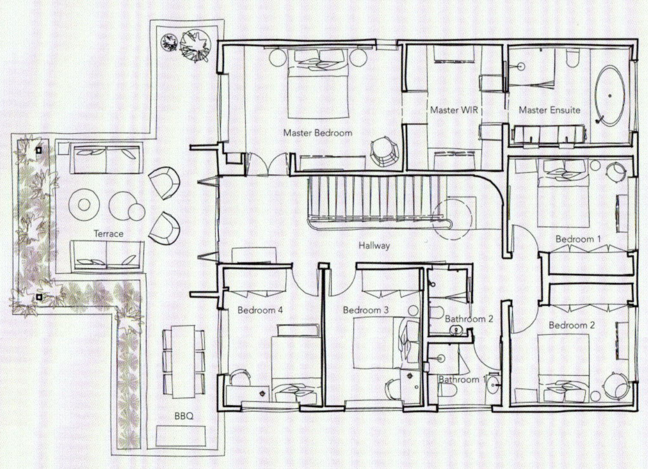

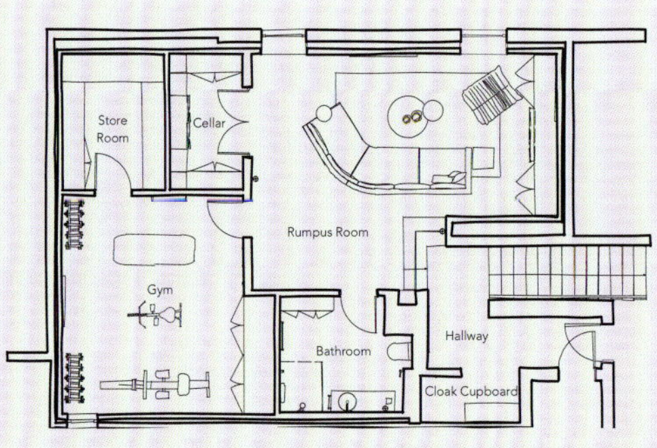

OPPOSITE: The architect's reinterpretation of the front of the house, with subtle Federation detailing. The square bay window brings light into the entrance hall.

INTERIOR DESIGN: KRISTIE NIXON
INTERIOR DECORATION: LUCY CARROLL & MADDIE HELYER
BUILDER: HORIZON

SKYLINE PENTHOUSE

The transformation of an apartment perched above a bustling streetscape

'I LOVE THE CHALLENGE OF INCORPORATING TRADITION INTO A CONTEMPORARY INTERIOR. IT BRINGS INTEREST AND WARMTH AND REFLECTS THE PERSONALITIES OF THE OWNERS, MAKING THE SPACE RICHER AND MORE AUTHENTIC.'

Double Bay is a harbourside suburb about 4 kilometres east of Sydney's central business district. It falls within the traditional lands of the Gadigal people and is part of the Eora Nation. This area has a rich Aboriginal history, evidenced by rock art and shell middens. It is also one of Sydney's prettiest and most glamorous suburbs, and is home to great restaurants, cafes, designer shops, leafy streets and popular beaches.

This penthouse apartment sits in the middle of Double Bay's village, but is high enough to escape the noise and bustle below. It was previously the home of relatives of the clients, whose preference was for a dark, moody interior. The new owners were determined to bring in a lighter, more colourful palette and make it their own.

Aware of the need to transform the apartment to align with their brief, we reconfigured the spaces to significantly change both the ambience of the interior and the function of spaces. The project took just nine months from concept to completion – quite remarkable, considering the complexities of working within a multistorey building with access off a narrow laneway.

The spine of the apartment is a lofty, generous corridor with a full-length skylight. We developed our concept around this feature by forming curved openings that determined the design language throughout. The curves were repeated in the bathrooms, the kitchen and living room, and helped to soften the otherwise austere angles. Two pairs of steel-framed glass doors, which lead to separate studies, allow light to pour into the corridor, which is now finished in a light, hand-waxed stucco.

The owners, who were downsizing from a larger home, have a collection of books that justified building library shelves in the main study. They were also bringing precious art and artifacts – mostly traditional pieces that reflect their history. I love the challenge of incorporating tradition into a contemporary interior. It brings interest and warmth and reflects the personalities of the owners, making the space richer and more authentic. And that, after all, is our aim. Into this mix, they added newly acquired large, abstract contemporary artworks that imbue the spaces with dynamic texture and colour.

The small but dramatic entry into the apartment is wrapped in a dark charcoal-green wallcovering, which is juxtaposed with a rich scarlet console and a cherished artwork. The corridor off the entry is defined by a timber portal leading into the contrasting light, bright spaces beyond. There is an intriguing glimpse of the sculptured travertine island bench as you walk through the corridor, past the two studies and the bedrooms. As you pass through a further timber portal, which defines the end of the corridor, the rich colours of the living room are revealed. The same travertine is sculpted and ribbed in a feature that houses the fireplace and conceals a television. The rich and vibrant tones of one of our rugs adds colour and texture to the room.

The most delightful element of this project was the trust that our clients placed in us. It turned an interesting design journey into a rich shared experience and helped us to deliver a home that they have a strong and lasting emotional connection with.

PREVIOUS: We introduced curves to the corridor, punctuated the walls with steel-and-glass doors and finished them in hand-waxed stucco. A hand-knotted silk rug adds warmth.

OPPOSITE: Timber portals define the entry to the kitchen and living room and offer a glimpse of the curved travertine island bench.

ABOVE: The dramatic dark wallcovering of the entry hall is offset by a deep raspberry Maxalto console and a treasured family painting.

OPPOSITE: We designed the bookshelves with openings for special objects and small paintings.

ABOVE: The study is lined with a deep-green wallcovering, giving a traditional atmosphere to this contemporary setting.

ABOVE: A combination of honed and carved Ocean Blue travertine conceals storage for audio-visual equipment, including a television on a lifting mechanism.

OPPOSITE: The Jo Davenport painting, commissioned by the clients, hangs behind the armchair by Gio Ponti in chartreuse velvet, which sits on one of our rugs.

DAVENPORT

PREVIOUS: Ocean Blue travertine was carved and shaped to create the island bench. The joinery behind follows its curves.

OPPOSITE: Shades of gold, blue and charcoal are layered to create a softly luxurious main bedroom.

ABOVE: Looking through the second small study off the corridor, which doubles as a spare bedroom, to an ensuite bathroom.

ABOVE: The bath is tucked into a curved alcove flanked by a wall of Ocean Blue travertine. The walls are finished in a custom shade of microcement that reflects the colour of the stone.

OPPOSITE: The language of curves is continued in the design of the travertine-topped vanity.

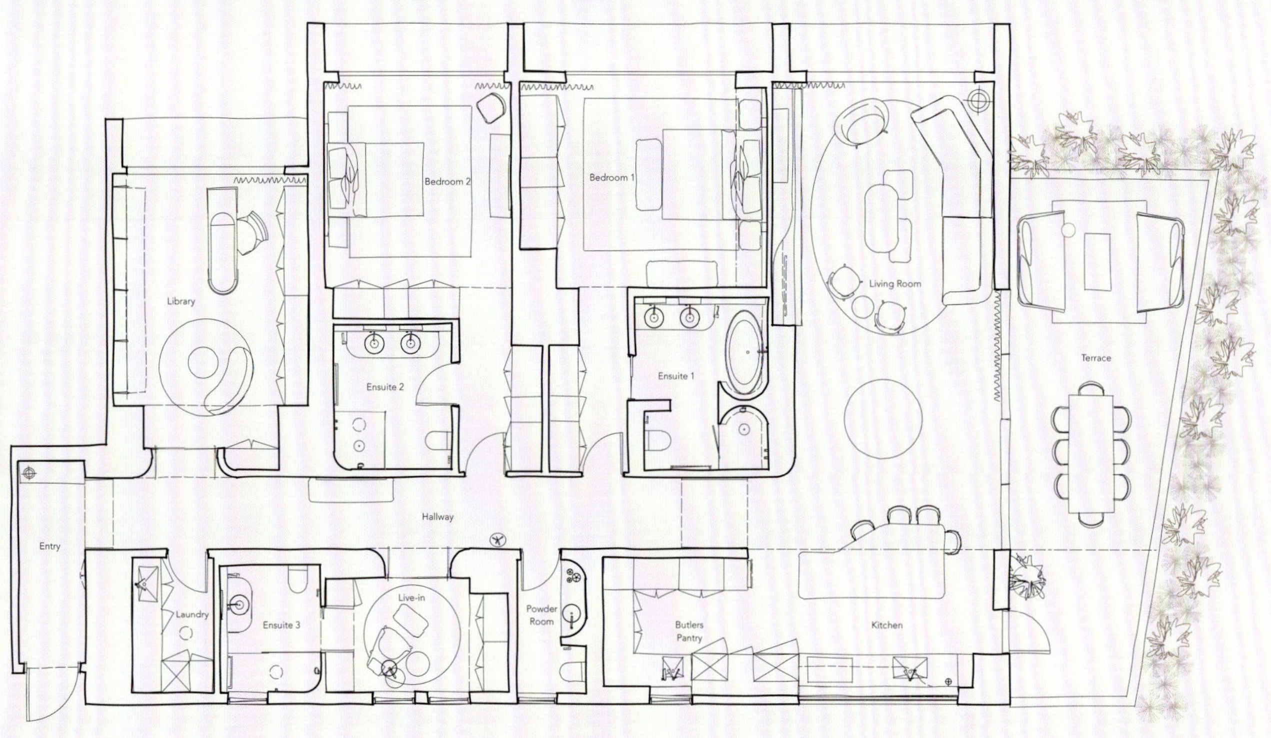

OPPOSITE: The walls of the terrace off the living room are painted in charcoal, creating a dramatic background for the plants.

INTERIOR DESIGN: CRISTINA REPETI
INTERIOR DECORATION: LUCY CARROLL
ARCHITECTURE: RICHARD COLE ARCHITECTURE
LANDSCAPE DESIGN: DANGAR BARIN SMITH
BUILDER: ROSSINGTON BUILDING CONTRACTORS

SADDLE HOUSE

The simple design aesthetic of an agricultural shed is the foundation for a palette of robust materials layered with rich tonal hues

'WHILE SIMPLE IN CONCEPT, THE HOME NEEDED TO BE EXTREMELY DURABLE AND ALIGNED WITH THE SURROUNDING LANDSCAPE.'

The town of Scone in the Upper Hunter Shire of New South Wales is known as the 'horse capital of Australia'. Originally home to the Wonnarua people, the traditional custodians of the land, it was first explored by Europeans in 1823. A village was established in 1826, and it is now surrounded by stud farms that are notable for breeding and raising thoroughbred racehorses.

Based on the design aesthetic of an agricultural shed, Saddle House is located on a working farm. It faces an extraordinary vista of saddle-shaped mountains – eerily appropriate in this rural setting. While simple in concept, the home needed to be extremely durable and aligned with the surrounding landscape.

Having worked with the owners on their Sydney home, we had a good grasp of their aesthetic, which included a love of art and natural textures. For this rural home, the basic materials of concrete, recycled blackbutt, steel and microcement were the foundation upon which we built a palette of colour and texture. Robust materials layered with the rich tonal colours of the furnishings reflect this rural lifestyle.

The raked ceilings create spaces that soar from a height of 2.6 metres to 3.5 metres in the main living area. The kitchen anchors this large room with a dining area and two sitting spaces – one orientated to the fireplace and the other to the gorgeous view. Rugs define the sitting spaces, and pendants determine the dining and kitchen areas.

Lighting these spaces was challenging, as downlights are largely ineffective in such high ceilings. My philosophy is that lighting should be purposeful – I see no point simply lighting the floor – so we used a combination of wall lights, pendants and floor lamps and put strip lighting in the working areas. The result is softly layered lighting scenes with highlights where required.

The entry to this home is defined by a solid, carved timber bench and a dark, rugged timber console. The entry is connected to a long corridor running the length of the house, which is punctuated with steel beams, timber doors and portals with low-level lighting and unglazed ceramic wall lights. A joinery 'box' defines the kitchen on one side, and we designed blackbutt and steel shelving for the corridor to display artefacts collected by the owners. The box also serves as a gallery for their collection of artworks. The access to bedrooms, bathrooms, a mud room and a steam room are along this corridor.

For the furnishings, we chose muted tones. In the main sitting room, we designed an artisanal coffee table made from salvaged telegraph poles, which sits on one of our rugs. A classic chair, which we had reupholstered in cowhide, reflects the nature of this property.

The exterior cladding of galvanised sheeting deflects the sun and protects the home from the elements. A timber deck wraps around the northern elevation, which, along with timber doors and rafters creates a stunning exterior for this beautiful rural property. This is a cohesive, finely detailed home that responds to its rural landscape with clarity and soul and applies sustainable principles in an elegant and timeless way.

PAGE 136: A large sculpture by David Ball is a focal point for this sitting area in a corner of the living room. Larrakitj poles by Djirrirra Wunungmurra Yukuwa tower calmly over the space.

PREVIOUS: The house is clad in zinc to withstand the elements – it will dull over time.

OPPOSITE: The view from the entry towards the main bedroom. A Riva 1920 Curve bench, cut from a single block of cedar, sits in the foreground.

ABOVE: The long corridor that runs the length of the house is punctuated by shelves in steel and recycled blackbutt.

PREVIOUS: In the main living area, the raked ceilings soar to 3.5 metres and open up to the view of the saddle-shaped mountains. Two seating areas are separated by a dining table.

ABOVE: Steel beams run from the interior to the edge of the terrace roof, which provides shade in summer.

OPPOSITE: The view from the living area to the main bedroom, and beyond to the landscape.

OPPOSITE: The walls and floor of the main ensuite are finished in microcement – a statement of simplicity.

ABOVE: A view of the surrounding farm and the mountains.

RIGHT: The sun catches the walls of the shower in the main bedroom's ensuite.

ABOVE LEFT: The entrance to the guest cloakroom is flanked by Gaypalani Wanambi's intricate engravings on repurposed road signs and scrap metal.

ABOVE RIGHT: Detail of one of the bedrooms, featuring a custom headboard against the back of the robe made from recycled blackbutt joinery.

OPPOSITE: The guest cloakroom also serves as a steam room. Unglazed Japanese terracotta mosaics and handmade wall lights reflect the colour of the raw earth surrounding the property.

OVERLEAF: Late afternoon sun softly lights the mountains and paddocks.

OPPOSITE: The mud room directly off the main outside entry houses the owners' working and polo gear.

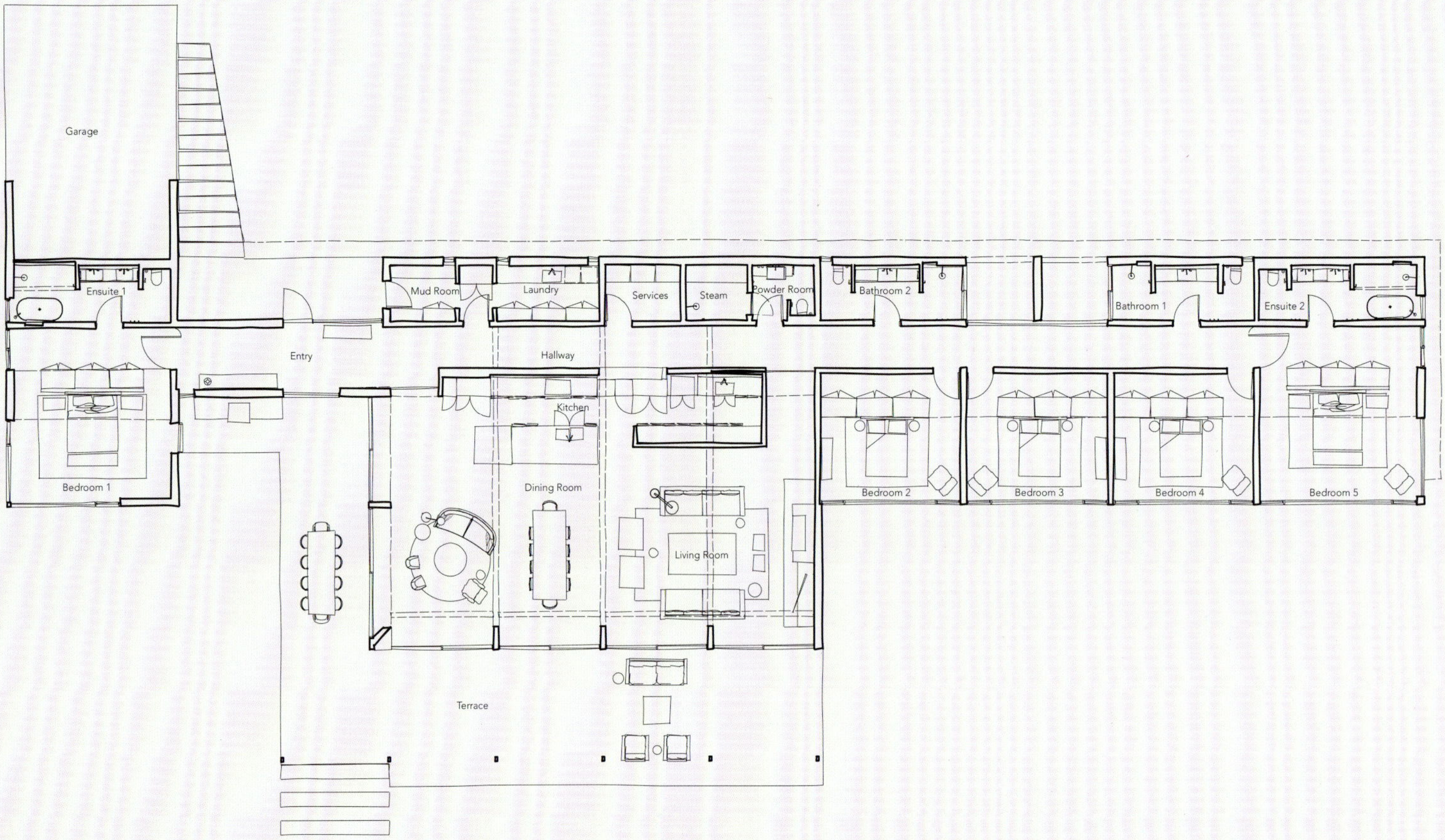

DESIGN INSIGHT: SCRIBBLE

A rug inspired by the iconic indigenous scribbly gum tree

If there was ever a perfect placement for this Hare + Klein rug, Scribble, it is this rural setting, where indigenous trees surround the homestead. The rug's designer, Kristie Nixon, was horse-riding in an area with an abundance of indigenous scribbly gums. She had always been intrigued by the graphic patterns in the bark of these trees, which are formed when old bark falls away to reveal the trails and burrows of the scribbly gum moths. She saw the potential to translate this feature of the Australian bush into a rug. It is an iconic image of the Australian bush that resonates with her and reflects the land she grew up on.

The design evolved from her detailed close-up photographs of the bark. She translated and reinterpreted the images, using digital software to bring the designs to life. The process of spinning, dyeing and knotting the Tibetan wool, hemp and silk by hand was a perfect vehicle for this design. It interprets the imperfect marks made by the moths beautifully.

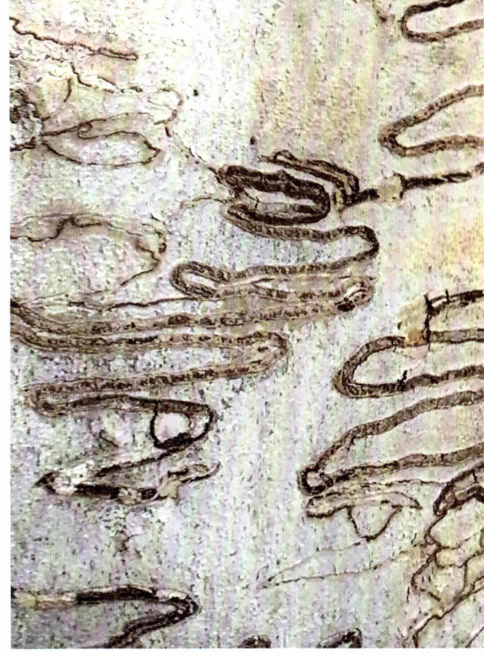

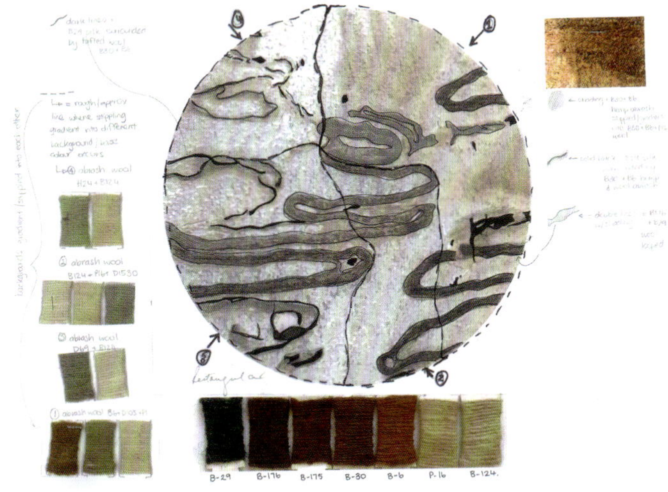

DESIGNER: KRISTIE NIXON
MANUFACTURED BY: DESIGNER RUGS AUSTRALIA
MANUFACTURING METHOD: HAND KNOTTING
MATERIALS: TIBETAN WOOL, HEMP, SILK

INTERIOR DESIGN & DECORATION: MERYL HARE
ARCHITECTURE: SPACEAGENCY
LANDSCAPE DESIGN: ROBERT FINNIE DESIGN
BUILDER: TALO CONSTRUCTION
ADDITIONAL PHOTOGRAPHY: RIDHWAAN MOOLLA

PEPPERMINT GROVE

The respectful preservation of a heritage home
for present-day living

'OUR APPROACH WAS TO CREATE ROOMS WITH PURPOSE: SPACES THAT LURE YOU IN WITH A PROMISE OF COMFORT, IN ALL SENSES.'

There is a fine line between preserving the integrity of a heritage property for contemporary living and destroying its original architectural language. It takes an owner with a keen sense of responsibility and respect for the original building to become its custodian. Having researched the history of Carbrakine House, the new owners were clear in their brief to us that they wanted to preserve and honour the architecture by keeping as many original features as possible.

Peppermint Grove is a western suburb of Perth that was named by European settlers for the indigenous peppermint tree that is endemic to the area. It was pastoral land until it was subdivided in 1891 and became a suburb. Carbrakine was built in about 1898. The design – an outstanding example of the Federation Queen Anne style – was commissioned by the prominent pastoralist Charles Lee-Steere and is attributed to Sir Joseph John Talbot Hobbs, a notable Western Australian architect. Sir Talbot Hobbs designed many prominent WA homes and buildings before he set off to Europe to join the armed forces in WWI, where he survived Gallipoli and the horrors of the Western Front, returning as Australia's highest-ranking soldier.

After WWI, Carbrakine House changed hands several times, eventually falling into disrepair. Substantial work was done shortly before the beginning of WWII. More recently, a brutalist extension was added that created a disconnect between old and new. Its heritage features were stripped back and a large concrete gallery was attached on the eastern side.

Alongside an architect and landscape architect, we took on the task of creating a warm and comfortable family home that would withstand the extremes of Perth's weather, while respecting the home's heritage. I love the challenge of working with committed owners to reinterpret a historic home, which is all about finding the right balance of history and contemporary living.

Details make all the difference between a 'nod' to the original architecture and complete disregard. With this philosophy in mind, we designed steel-and-glass doors that replicate the shape of the original decorative timber arches of the verandahs and maintain the connection between spaces. They also serve the purpose, when opened and closed, of maintaining optimal heating and cooling in this extreme climate. The rooms of this home boast high ceilings – some with intact cornices – and beautifully proportioned bay windows to both the north and west.

The original wandoo floors – *Eucalyptus wandoo* is a native Western Australian gum tree – were stripped back and retained, and portals constructed of the same timber, frame the new glass-and-steel doors. The original floating staircase – the first to be constructed in Western Australia – was luckily still in excellent condition.

Our approach was to create rooms with purpose: spaces that lure you in with a promise of comfort, in all senses. The London room, named by the owners for a previous home, with its quirky art, contemporary sofas and a pair of antique Japanese chests that frame the original fireplace, is a gorgeous space. It is enhanced with a textured grass-cloth wallcovering that adds warmth and contrast. Added layers of texture, colour and art contribute to the fine design detailing, creating an aesthetically pleasing balance.

The kitchen planning included creating a partly concealed butler's pantry that hides the messy food preparation, allowing us to showcase the beautiful front kitchen that faces the living, dining and terrace areas.

A large hall connects the entry to the southern verandah. This space needed a purpose to prevent it from becoming cold and unwelcoming, so we created a small sitting area near the front door and a casual reading area that overlooks the pool. Next to this is a playful family room. The connection between these spaces is articulated by another set of steel-framed arched doors.

When the project was complete, the owners sent us a heartfelt note: 'First, I owe you an apology. When I said, "A house is really just a house, I'm not sure it really makes you happier", you responded, "Of course it does." I can now say, fully settled into Peppermint Grove, that I have never felt so comfortable, relaxed and inspired in a house in my entire life. I absolutely love it and find myself not wanting to leave. It is the most incredible experience living in such a stunning home. So, you were right. It's transformational!'

PAGE 158: The original 'floating' staircase that dominates the large entrance hall is in perfect condition.

PREVIOUS: Connecting steel-and-glass doors open up the spaces between the entry, the family room, and the pool and garden.

ABOVE: The view from the dining room of the London room, which features original architectural detailing.

OPPOSITE: The connections between the central and adjacent spaces are generous, and the original wandoo floorboards unify the rooms.

ABOVE LEFT: An Arthur Boyd painting of the Shoalhaven River hangs above the original fireplace surround.

ABOVE RIGHT: A detail of the room showing one of the matching pair of Japanese chests beneath the window.

ABOVE LEFT: Two Spanish easy chairs by Fredericia are placed in a cosy corner under the staircase near the entry.

ABOVE RIGHT: We lined the walls with a grass-cloth wallcovering, offsetting the painting by Marise Maas above the Minotti sofa.

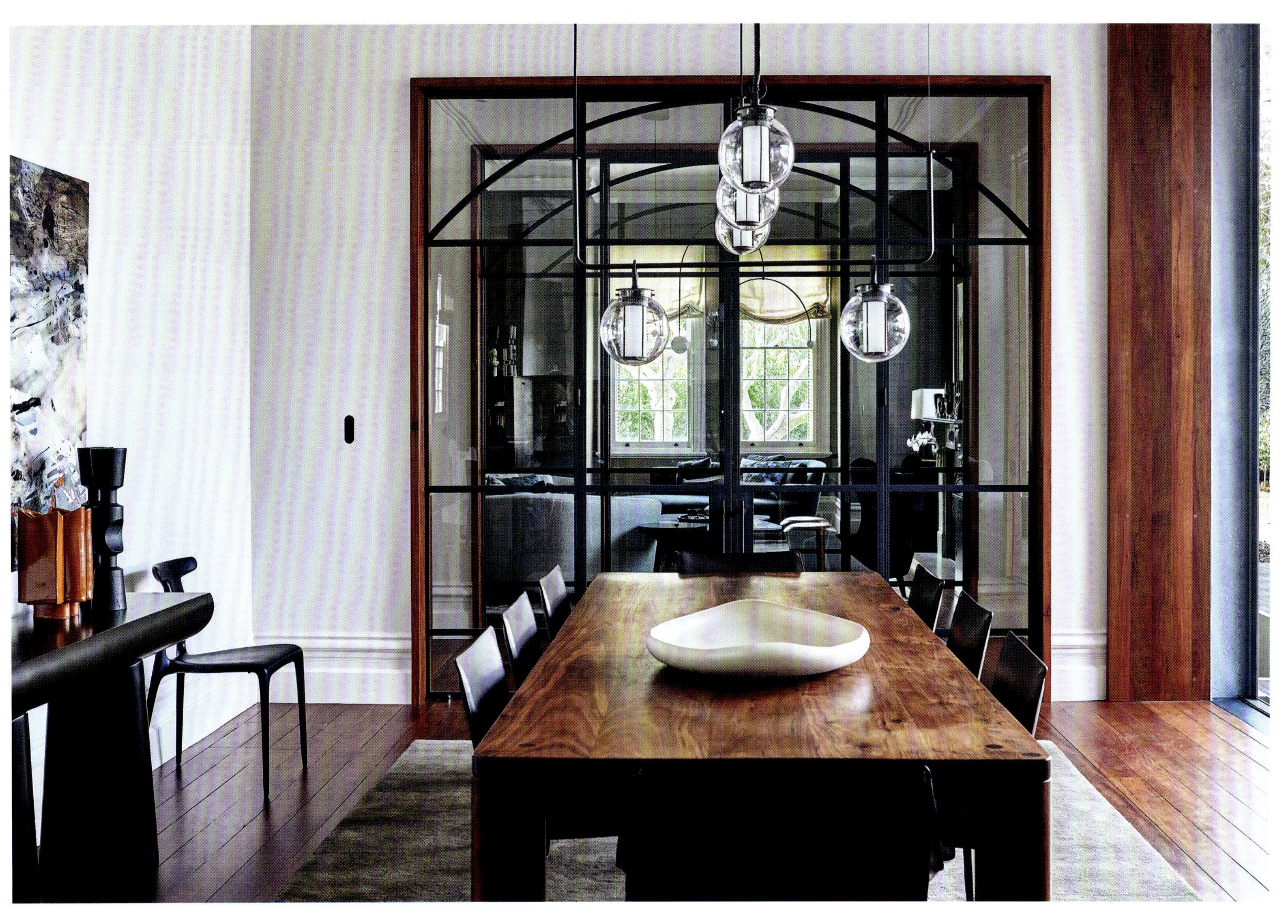

OPPOSITE: The view from the London room through two pairs of steel-and-glass doors to the dining area and kitchen.

ABOVE: The dining area connects to the beautifully landscaped terrace and outdoor seating.

OVERLEAF: A view of the kitchen from the dining table with the butler's pantry and wine store behind. Rilio marble features on the back kitchen bench and the splashback, and the extractor is concealed by the curved hood finished in hand-waxed stucco.

OPPOSITE: The child's room is spacious and playful – a study area has been inserted into the bay and a variety of textures and colours create interest.

ABOVE: A flexible concertina pleated screen in deep russet creates a sense of privacy for the bed.

ABOVE: Light pours into the main bedroom from three directions, adding to the feeling of spaciousness. Sisal carpeting and layered bedding add warmth and colour.

OPPOSITE: We designed a dressing area behind the timber bedhead, which is finished in pleated linen and velvet.

OPPOSITE: The main ensuite vanity was designed as a furniture piece, rather than being built in. The bath is nestled into a timber-panelled alcove, giving the room a connection to its past.

ABOVE: We designed a slab of silver travertine that cantilevers across two tall windows and holds a Nood Co charcoal concrete basin. Two Ruth Levine totems and a small Pierre-Auguste Renoir sketch embellish this guest cloakroom.

ABOVE: The architects elevated the pool to remove the need for a fence.

LEFT: The partly shaded outdoor terrace features a seating platform and an open courtyard softly surrounded with timber privacy screening.

OPPOSITE: An outdoor shower against the concrete garden wall is almost sculptural in relief.

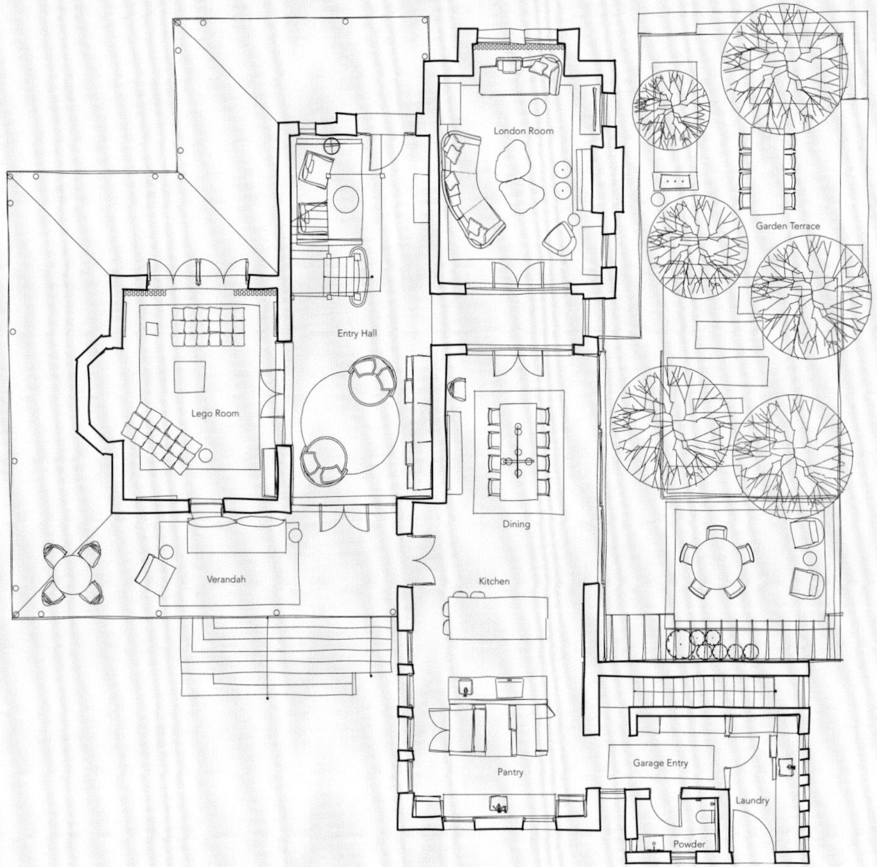

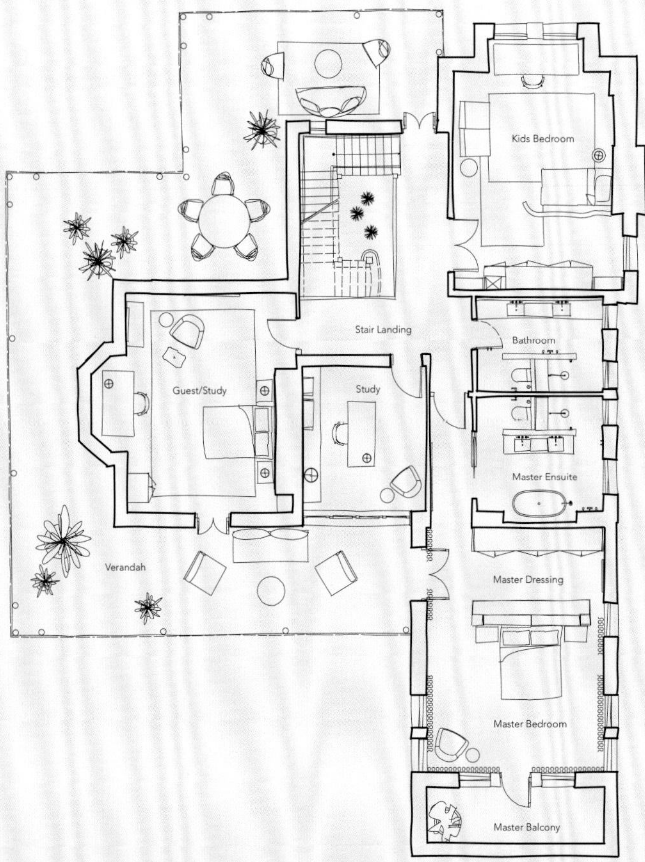

OPPOSITE: The front entry features original timber detailing and local Western Australian sandstone, framed by an established frangipani tree.

INTERIOR

DESIGN INSIGHT: CONNECTING ARCHES

The design of visual links that respect heritage and connect spaces

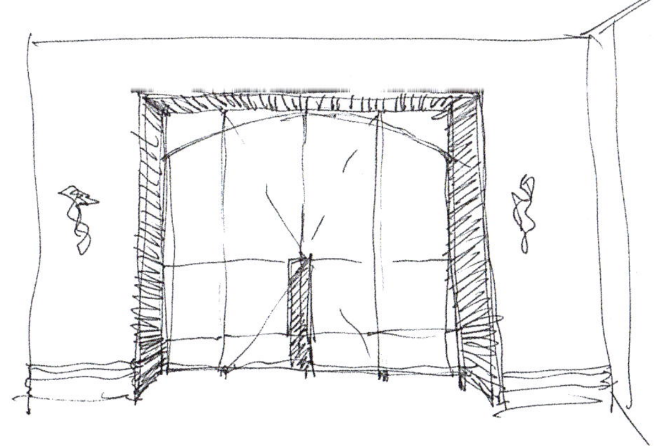

At the onset of a project there is often an 'aha' moment that steers the design aesthetic. I had one of those on the plane when I was returning to Sydney after my first visit to the Peppermint Grove house.

I knew it was imperative to link the spaces visually, especially on the ground level, but they also had to be individually climate controlled to mitigate Perth's extreme weather. The distinct shape of the arched trims on the verandahs that dominate the exterior of this beautiful heritage-listed home inspired the shape of the interleading doors, and the use of steel and glass allowed a visual link.

My original sketch was primitive, but it set the tone for the respectful renovation of the home. Further exploration of this idea continued, using 3D imagery to model the linking of the rooms and spaces. Detailed construction drawings were documented and submitted to the manufacturer. The doors were made in Perth and fitted within timber portals made from the same local timber that graces the floors throughout. This simple idea was an integral element of the overall reinterpretation of this home.

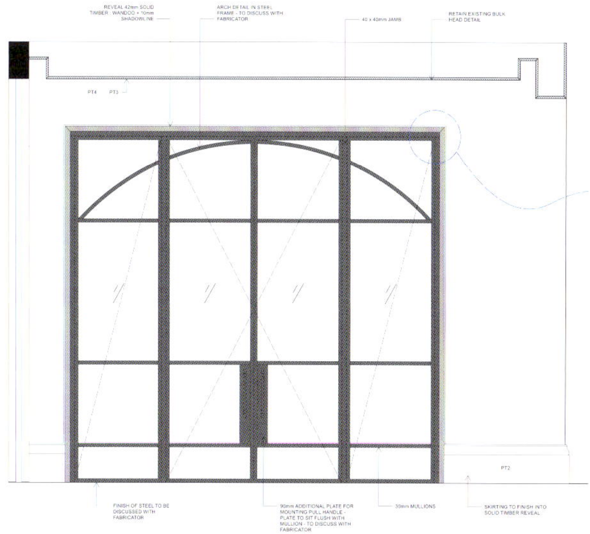

DESIGNER: MERYL HARE

MANUFACTURED BY: ENVISAGE WA

MATERIALS: STEEL, GLASS, TIMBER REVEAL

INTERIOR DESIGN: CRISTINA REPETI
INTERIOR DECORATION: LUCY CARROLL & MADDIE HELYER

OCEAN FRONT

A blank canvas is redefined as a vibrant home
that reflects its coastal setting

'THE COLOUR PALETTE ... LEADS YOU ON AN INTRIGUING JOURNEY, FROM THE OCEAN TONES AT THE FRONT OF THE HOME TO THE MORE GROUNDED HUES OF THE LANDSCAPE AT THE BACK.'

I first met the owners of this home some time ago – it has taken several years of planning and building to finally see their home transformed. Architecturally, the home is not significant. What was more relevant to the owners was that the interior supported the way they wanted to live and respected what was important to them and their young family.

The house is in a lovely location in the Newcastle area of New South Wales, on a level block that overlooks the beach. Starting with an almost blank canvas, we redefined the living areas and created new spaces for the family that have a lived-in ambience, reflecting their taste. Colour was a big factor in our overall concept. As well as rich tones that respond to the surrounding landscape, the owners wanted a vibrant home that reflected their delightfully quirky taste in art. The colour palette of these newly linked spaces leads you on an intriguing journey, from the ocean tones at the front of the home to the more grounded hues of the landscape at the back.

The kitchen is at the heart of the living space. Along with shades of deep blue-grey and the softness of the oak timber, we introduced a language of soft curves, bronze metal and beautiful slabs of Vagli marble on pale-grey porcelain floor tiles to define this area.

In the living room, the timber floor was retained and it now forms a foundation for an elegant but relaxed seating area. New joinery houses a fireplace and creates a feature on the entry side. The floorplan acknowledges this feature as the focal point of this room, while also embracing the view of the ocean. One of our hand-knotted rugs introduces colour and pattern, and reflects the owners' collection of ceramics and other treasures.

The transition through to the dining area is twofold. It can be accessed or shut off from the kitchen with concealed sliding doors. If these are left open, there is a direct connection to the ocean view. Alternatively, the dining area can be approached via the passage that terminates with intriguing curved joinery that gives a glimpse of the colourful family room. The custom pendant over the dining table is a subtle reflection of the curves of the table's base, and a repetition of our design language of curves that is repeated in the fireplace in the family room.

In the main bedroom suite upstairs, we've introduced a calm and soft palette of colour and texture. This room faces the ocean and includes a private lounging area that is perfect for whale watching or just contemplating the lovely view. It's a comfortable and private parents' retreat.

There is an element of surprise when you arrive at the entry of the home. The exterior doesn't prepare you for the warm, homely and richly coloured interior. It surprises and delights both the family and their friends in a way that they couldn't have imagined when we started on this journey with them.

Toddler to Table

PAGE 184: This confluence of spaces is defined by subtle curves and the transition of floor finishes.

PREVIOUS: The soft curves of the joinery are evident in the view from the front living room.

OPPOSITE: We designed the kitchen with an eat-in table for everyday family meals.

ABOVE: Vagli marble, blue-grey slatted timber and oak define this area of the kitchen, which is the centre of the home.

OPPOSITE: This vista from the dining area can be closed off with sliding doors or left open to enjoy the view.

ABOVE: This joinery forms a 'full stop' to the entry passage by curving round to partly obscure the family room.

OVERLEAF: The fireplace, with its quirky collection of objects and art, is the focal point of this vibrant family room.

OPPOSITE: The main bedroom on the upper floor is designed as a calm retreat with layers of soft and luxurious textures.

ABOVE LEFT: This delightful sitting area is part of the main bedroom and faces the ocean.

ABOVE RIGHT: The ensuite adjacent to the main bedroom is a perfect place to soak up the view.

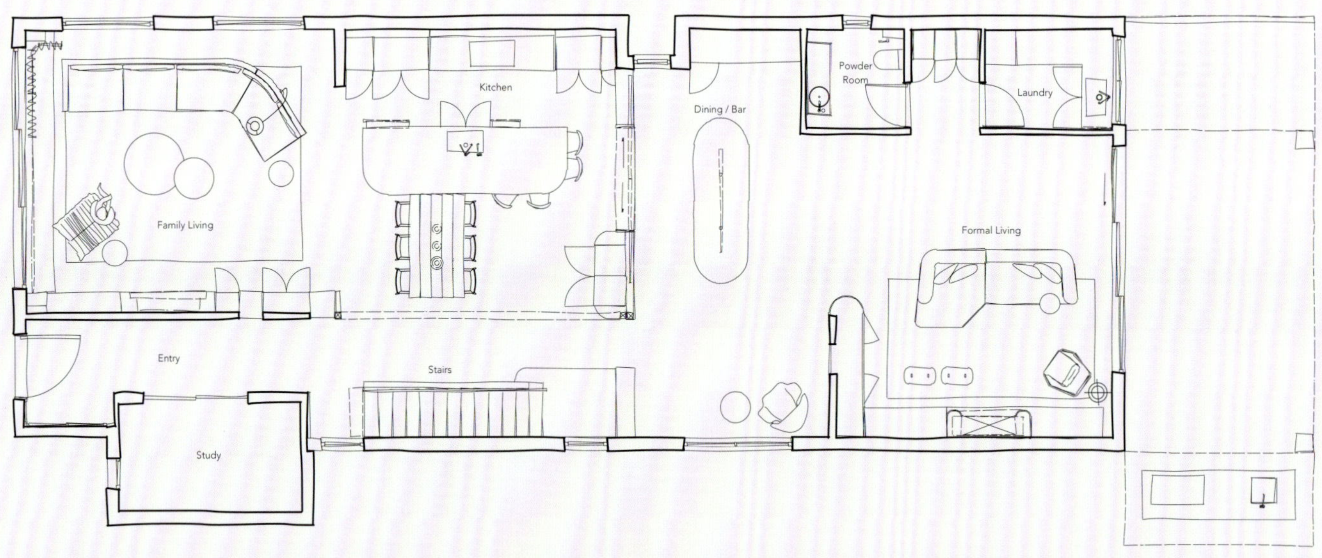

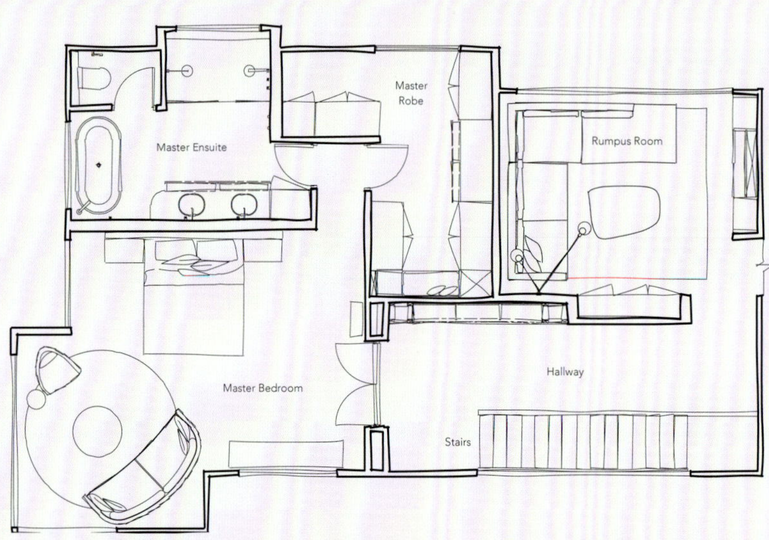

OPPOSITE: This corner of the living room features a Togo chair that creates a casual ambience, which is punctuated by the colourful Shuffle side table by &Tradition.

DESIGN INSIGHT: BRIDGE TABLE

A dining table inspired by the design of the Sydney Harbour Bridge

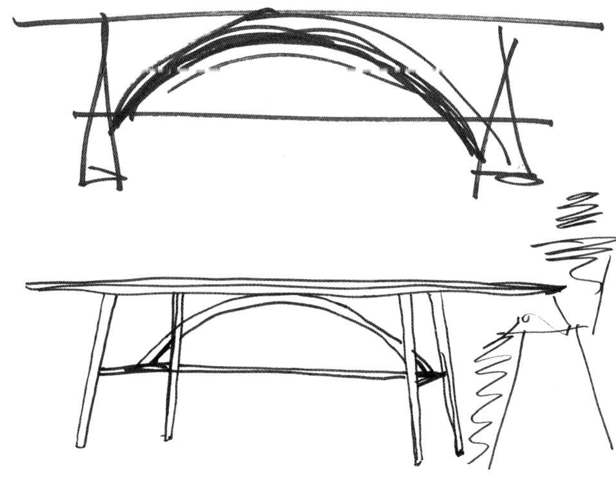

Early one morning, on my walk down to the Blues Point Reserve at McMahons Point in North Sydney, I watched the sun rise behind the Sydney Harbour Bridge. In that light, the structure of the bridge was strikingly clear and, in another 'aha' moment, the shape of its arches and supporting pylons became the inspiration for the Bridge Table. I sketched it from that simple idea and shape.

Given that tables have been fashioned since humans lived in caves, the challenge was to design a dining table that had a sense of place and originality and also captured our aesthetic. Working with the manufacturer – particularly on the joint where the arches meet the crossbar – was critical to refining the design. This respectful collaboration with makers is an integral part of our approach.

The table is made locally from sustainable timbers, meaning it has low embodied energy – in line with the philosophy of our practice, and it is designed to last. To protect the concept's originality, the design was successfully registered with IP Australia. In 2021 it won a Good Design Award Gold Winner for Design Excellence.

Bridge Table fits perfectly in the dining area of this home. It replicates the smooth flowing lines of the interiors and relates to the ocean in a subtle way. We paired it with Scandinavian-designed chairs with curved backrests.

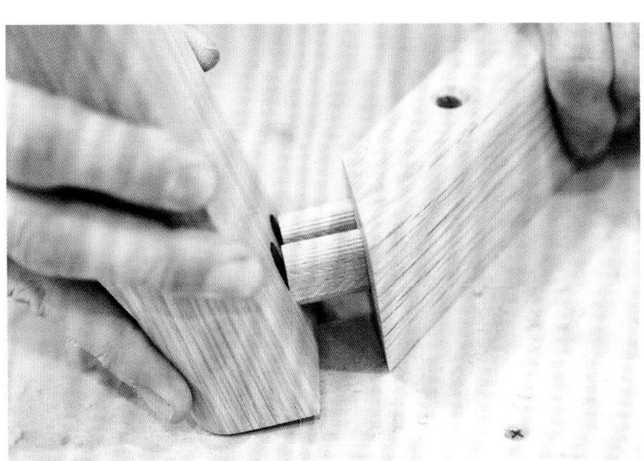

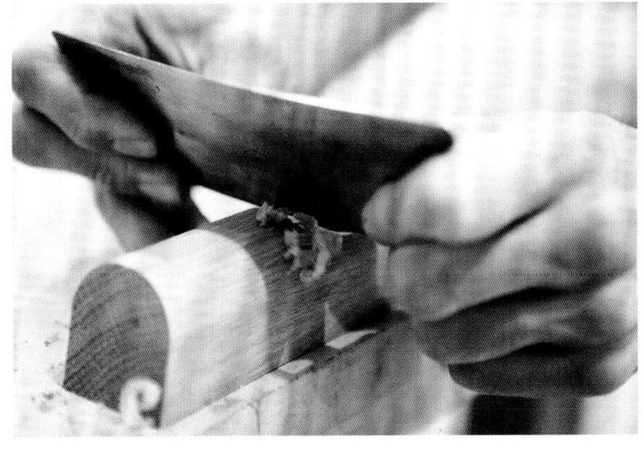

DESIGNER: MERYL HARE
MANUFACTURED: SYDNEY
MATERIALS: AMERICAN OAK OR WALNUT
PHOTOGRAPHER, IMAGE OPPOSITE: ANSON SMART

INTERIOR DESIGN: CRISTINA REPETI
INTERIOR DECORATION: LUCY CARROLL
ARCHITECTURE: TKD ARCHITECTS & R2 STUDIOS
LANDSCAPE DESIGN: GARDEN LIFE
BUILDER: GROSSER CONSTRUCTIONS

MANDEMAR

A generous and welcoming rural home is flooded with light from every direction, creating delightful winter and summer spaces

'IN TIME, THE HOUSE WILL BE SURROUNDED BY TREES ... SELECTED CAREFULLY FOR THEIR COLOURS, SCENT AND CANOPY.'

Mandemar is a small village in Wingecarribee Shire, in the Southern Highlands region of New South Wales. This new home was a passion project for our client. He oversaw every part of the process, from planning, documenting and building right through to selecting all the furniture and furnishings. Tragically, he didn't live to see it completed. It is with a very heavy heart that I have included it in this book as a tribute to him and the dream home he planned.

The house is built on a farm, perched just below the brow of a hill and overlooks the beautiful surrounding landscape. At the time we photographed Mandemar, the landscaping hadn't had time to establish. In time, the house will be surrounded by trees that our client selected carefully for their colours, scent and canopy.

Light floods into this home from every direction and the planning of rooms and their function takes this into account. The winter lounge faces north and west, ensuring that this cosy room will benefit from the sun in winter. The main living, dining and kitchen area faces south and has smaller windows and doors to the east and west, meaning it will be cooler in the summer months.

In this large room, we have placed the furniture in zones, both to break up the space and also to allow the residents to enjoy the different aspects. The main seating faces the fireplace and the trophy deer, affectionately known as Winston. The dining table splits the room, leaving the smaller seating zone on the other side, oriented towards the view.

The kitchen, which is finished in rich timber and bronze, features a substantial concealed butler's pantry, perfect for catering to large gatherings. Across the hallway is my favourite room – the powder room. It's warm in colour and texture, generous in scale and showcases one of our client's many quirky paintings.

This is a well-considered rural home that will grow into itself over time. The Hare + Klein team are very proud to have been instrumental in bringing the project to completion in very difficult circumstances, along with the architect, builders and landscape designers.

PAGE 202: The Ewoud de Groot painting over the fireplace was one of the client's favourites.

PAGES 204–205: The kitchen was positioned to allow the cook to enjoy the view. The pivot door on the right conceals a sizeable butler's pantry, intended for catering for large gatherings.

PREVIOUS: The intimate sitting area features layers of textures and colours that reflect the landscape outside.

ABOVE: The main sitting area embraces the fireplace, the television, two paintings by Charmaine Pwerle, and Winston the deer.

OPPOSITE: The view from the sitting area to the raised entry hall, which features an artwork by the French painter Pierre-Marie Brisson.

VILLAS

PREVIOUS: The pendant light over the dining table was custom designed and made by Sabu Studio to provide soft light over the table without obstructing the view.

OPPOSITE: The winter lounge is bathed in morning sun and overlooks the paddocks to the east of the home. This is a cosy room designed for winter evenings around the fire.

ABOVE: The eastern elevation of the home.

ABOVE: Two details of the main ensuite bathroom – the finishes were selected for their practicality and simple aesthetic.

OPPOSITE: The bath sits on a raised platform and overlooks a planting of trees that will, in time, provide a privacy screen.

ABOVE: The headboard partly conceals a passage to the robes and the door to the ensuite.

ABOVE & RIGHT: A generous space was allocated to the guest cloakroom, which has a separate toilet and double trough sinks in marble. The quirky sheep painting by Stephanie Brancatisano that is reflected in the mirror brings humour to the room.

PAGE 219: The terrace leading off the kitchen is furnished around the outdoor fireplace.

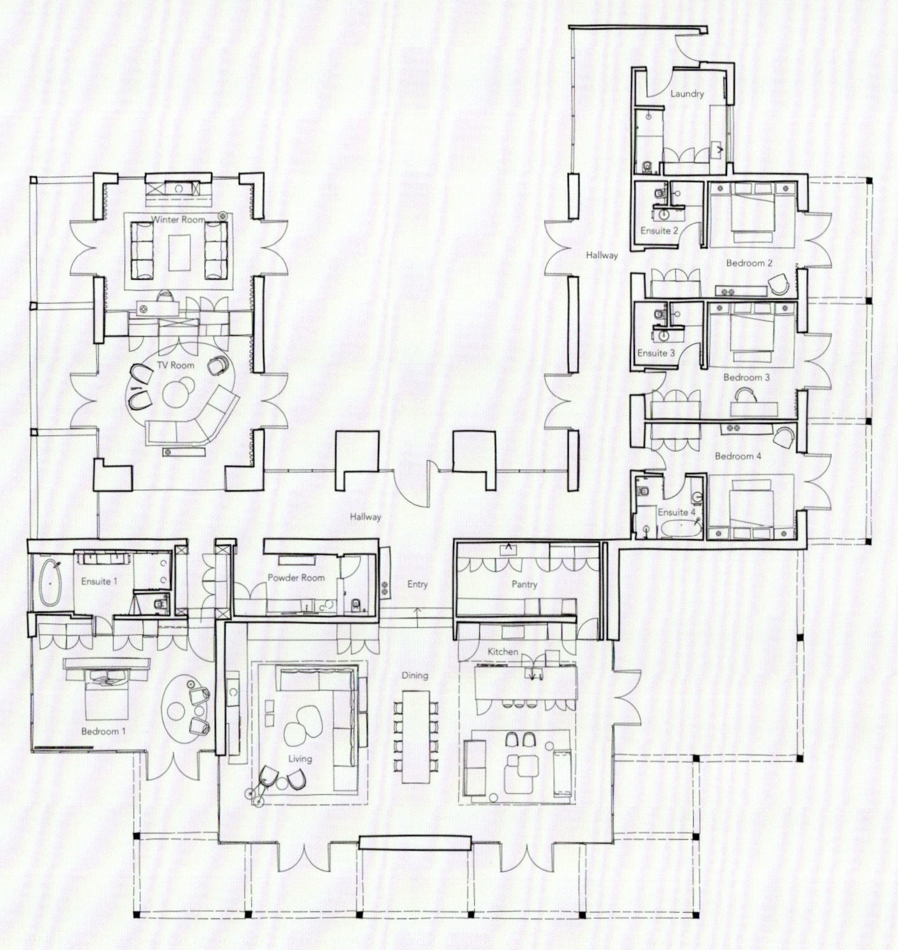
Laundry
Winter Room
Hallway
Ensuite 2
Bedroom 2
TV Room
Ensuite 3
Bedroom 3
Bedroom 4
Ensuite 4
Hallway
Ensuite 1
Powder Room
Entry
Pantry
Kitchen
Dining
Bedroom 1
Living

INTERIOR DESIGN & DECORATION: MERYL HARE & CRISTINA REPETI
ARCHITECTURE: CORBEN ARCHITECTS
BUILDER: SANDLIK
ADDITIONAL PHOTOGRAPHY: TOM FERGUSON

HARBOURSIDE RESIDENCE

A collaboration with the architects brought contemporary relevance to a gloomy 1920s home

1,000 PLACES TO SEE BEFORE YOU DIE
THE SKETCH BOOK
HARE + KLEIN

'THE ORIGINAL STAIRCASE WAS REIMAGINED AS A SCULPTURAL FORM THAT GRACEFULLY ENHANCES THE ENTRY SPACE.'

This house on Cremorne Point overlooking Sydney Harbour is in a heritage conservation area. It was built around 1922, with additions and alterations approved in 1946. The original interior was gloomy and retained many of its interwar details, such as dark timber panelling, small rooms and outdated facilities. The new owners knew that they couldn't change the exterior, but they did want a contemporary, light-filled home that was relevant to their lifestyle.

The home had the potential to be transformed, so we embarked on a collaborative journey with the architects to redesign the interior. Starting from the entry, new timber floors were laid in a herringbone pattern that continues throughout the house. Simple joinery forms a plinth-like shape under a new curved window, and the original staircase was reimagined as a sculptural form that gracefully enhances the entry space.

The original floorplan was retained, but openings have been widened to allow light to flow from the south-western entry to the north-east harbour-front. This connection between front and back is enhanced with simple steel-framed doors that can close off the kitchen and dining areas. Steel is a recurring theme, punctuating the joinery throughout and forming portals between rooms.

The kitchen was designed as the centrepiece of the home. Exquisite slabs of blue-grey limestone define the area, which has an abundance of filtered natural light. The floor-to-ceiling joinery in blond veneer acts as a quiet backdrop to the limestone island and splashback, allowing it to shine. It is a functional space that makes cooking a joy for the owners.

We took advantage of the north-eastern aspect and harbour views by creating two dining areas – one for the family in the open kitchen and another in the more formal living area. Both open onto the covered verandah, where a serene view of the water is softly framed by trees. The transition from the new interior to the traditional detailing of the verandah is seamlessly expressed with contemporary furniture that complements the living rooms.

Upstairs, the main suite was reconfigured to include a walk-in robe that connects visually with a small study area and the view beyond. Soft drapes, a silk rug and a glamorous bathroom complete the suite, with a rich palette of furnishings and simple but beautifully detailed joinery. On the lower level, a small wine cellar and newly landscaped gardens complete the makeover of this heritage home.

PREVIOUS: A steel portal defines the opening between the original formal lounge and a sun room – now joined as one space with a fireplace, creating a small, cosy seating area.

OPPOSITE: The original facade now boasts a new front door and side panels in glass and steel that bring light into the entry. A dramatic painting by Sophie Cape dominates this space.

ABOVE: The new curved window reflects the exterior curves, which are further emphasised by the Curve bench in blackened oak and the sculptural shapes of the staircase.

ABOVE: Details of the reconfigured staircase that gracefully enhances this space, juxtaposed with a steel blade shelving unit that creates an intriguing visual foil.

ABOVE LEFT: The view from the first-floor landing down to the living room.

ABOVE RIGHT: The original leadlight windows on the landing and the Apparatus Median pendant complement this eclectic space.

PREVIOUS: The east-facing first-level balcony is a lovely setting to enjoy the tranquil view of Mosman Bay.

OPPOSITE: Elegant Grey marble wraps around the island bench and splashbacks, creating a dramatic focal point to the kitchen.

ABOVE: Folding doors open to reveal an appliance pantry in the highly detailed kitchen.

ABOVE: The Modo chandelier delineates the casual round dining table – Patricia Urquiola's Asterias, one of my favourites, here in grey oak.

OPPOSITE: A corner of the living room featuring timber and steel shelving joinery, with the informal eating area in the background.

LANDSCAPE
ANDREW MARTIN INTERIOR DESIGN REVIEW VOL. 24

OPPOSITE: The main bedroom dressing room joinery in Eveneer Fango is flooded with natural light that flows through the steel blade shelving unit, which is a recurring feature throughout the home.

ABOVE: A corner of the bedroom doubles as a small study and dressing table.

OPPOSITE: The owners travel extensively and wanted a glamorous bathroom. We used contrasting marble with touches of bronze to add a luxury feel.

ABOVE: The generous bay window in the main bedroom faces Mosman Bay and forms the roof of the balcony below.

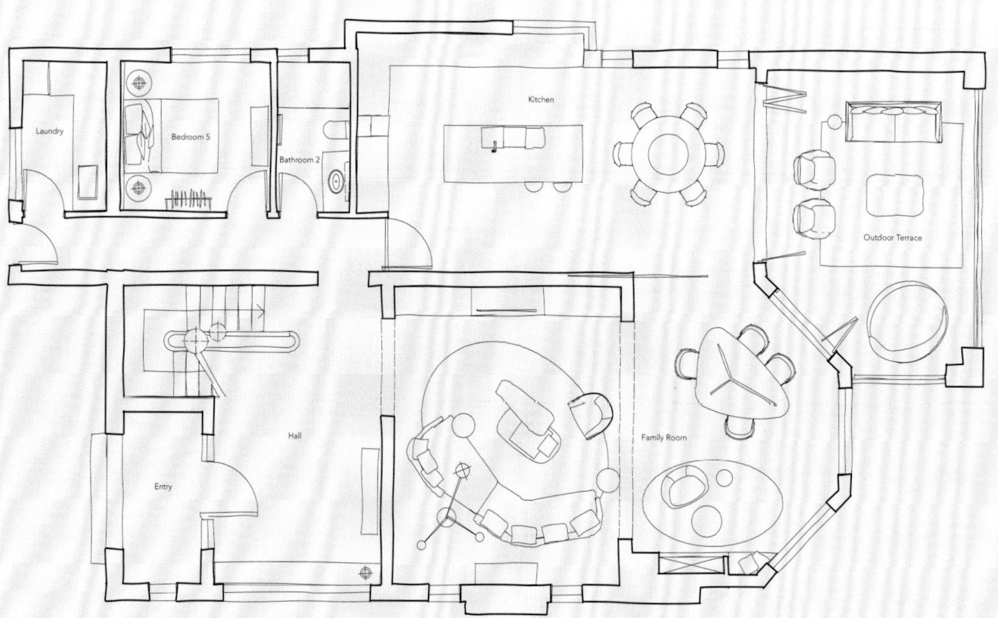

OPPOSITE: Sliding steel-framed doors separate the formal and casual dining areas.

INTERIOR DESIGN & DECORATION: MERYL HARE
BUILDER: STRATTI BUILDING
PHOTOGRAPHY: ANSON SMART

EDGE HOUSE

Perched on the edge of a cliff, this 1930s home warranted a youthful makeover awash with pink hues

'THESE DIVIDERS ARE JUST ONE EXAMPLE OF THE CIRCLES AND CURVES WE INTRODUCED AS A VISUAL FOIL TO THE SQUARE ARCHITECTURAL ENVELOPE.'

Our clients' original intention was to undertake substantial renovations and additions to Edge House. It was built in the 1930s and had endured some ad hoc alterations that had no flow and defied logic. The house is in an amazing location – literally perched on the edge of a cliff, overlooking the Pacific Ocean on one side and world-famous Bondi Beach on the other – so it certainly warranted a makeover. However, after costing such major works, they realigned their vision to concentrate on the interior.

Our task was to make the best use of the existing spaces without increasing the footprint. The original floorplan was outdated. There was an enclosed kitchen, a steep and tight staircase that you almost fell onto at the front door, and the main bedroom was literally squashed into a low, tight space in a converted loft. Luckily, the plain, square architectural envelope made our plans to reinvent the house's spaces and functions relatively uncomplicated.

The owners, who are keen cooks and love to entertain, requested a beautiful and functional kitchen in a prominent position in the living area, near the terrace. We demolished storage areas and a laundry to create the new kitchen and repurposed the original kitchen as a wine cellar and guest cloakroom. We also ventured out to the terrace, designing a pizza oven with a custom champagne cooler that is perfect for entertaining on a summer evening while overlooking the ever-changing Pacific Ocean.

The main bedroom suite required a more constructive approach. To create higher ceilings and make this part of the home liveable, it was necessary to replace and raise the roof. We installed one window that takes advantage of the view of the ocean from the bed and another that overlooks the beach. An infrared sauna was incorporated into the new ensuite and the dressing room was customised to suit the owners' needs.

The children's bedroom is both playful and practical. Two small bedrooms were opened up to form one big room that is partially divided by the custom bunk beds in the centre, creating individual spaces with operable portholes between them. Each child has their own space and can close off their beds, or they can play together. These dividers are just one example of the circles and curves we introduced as a visual foil to the square architectural envelope.

This is a vibrant family with two young children, so the design has a playfulness and vitality that suits their lifestyle. They had a strong preference for the colour pink, which we used in shades from deep crimson to soft pastels and everything inbetween. It is referenced in marble, joinery, furniture and furnishings, sometimes boldly, and sometimes subtly.

The pink theme is just one of the unconventional and quirky aspects of this reinvented home. It now exudes warmth and youth and houses an eclectic and confident art collection.

PREVIOUS: The entry staircase was redesigned to create a generous space that is dominated by the Ettore Sottsass mirror artwork.

OPPOSITE: A rug designed by Louise Olsen was chosen as floor artwork for the living room.

ABOVE: The climate-controlled wine cellar is an extension of the living room and showcases the owners' collection of champagne and wine.

PLENTY
LAROUSSE
OTTOLENGHI FLAVOUR
PERFECT FINISH

PREVIOUS: The kitchen benchtop and splashback are finished in Breccia Capraia Royal marble. The curved sofa in claret velvet is in keeping with the owners' preference for shades of pink.

OPPOSITE: As the owners love cooking, we specified a stainless-steel benchtop for the 'working side' of the kitchen. The rangehood and overhead cupboards are finished in Axolotl Pearl Patina.

ABOVE: The banquette seating around a custom oak dining table is the main interior dining space.

OPPOSITE: The outdoor entertaining area is punctuated by the pizza oven that we built in and attached to a concrete preparation bench.

ABOVE & RIGHT: The setting is spectacular – the Pacific Ocean is a backdrop to both indoor and outdoor living.

ABOVE: Now you see me, now you don't! The sliding panel in the round opening gives the children the option to connect – or not!

OPPOSITE: Two small bedrooms were turned into one large room for the children, with a specially designed bunk bed arrangement that gives them extra space to play.

ABOVE: The main bedroom's ensuite incorporates a concealed sauna, creating a compact wellness room. The tones of pink in the finishes are more subtle here.

OPPOSITE: The glamorous powder room on the ground level has a vanity clad in Tiberio marble, the owners' antique wall sconce and an asymmetric mirror.

OPPOSITE: The new window in the main bedroom frames a spectacular view of the ocean.

ABOVE: Detailed joinery in the dressing room that overlooks Bondi Beach.

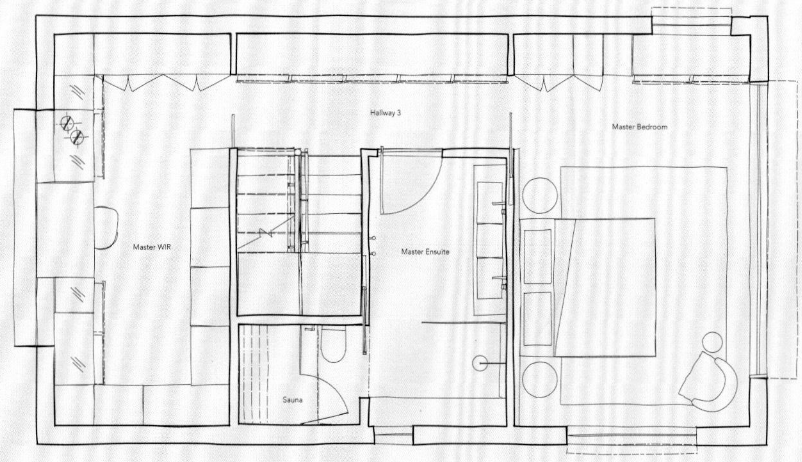

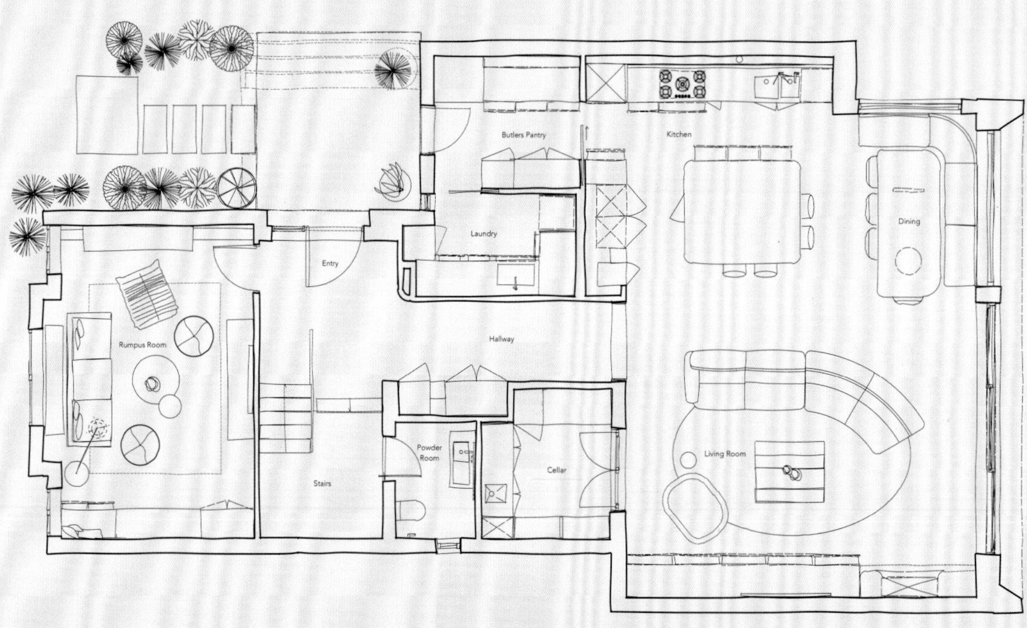

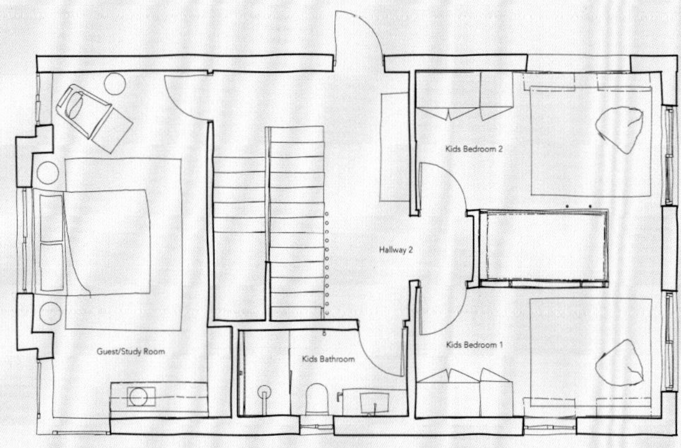

OPPOSITE: View back to the staircase from the living room, with a metal wall sculpture by Dion Horstmans and a circular artwork by Jo Bertini in the background.

INTERIOR DESIGN: CRISTINA REPETI
INTERIOR DECORATION: OWNER & SOUCIE HORNER
ARCHITECTURE: STAFFORD ARCHITECTURE
LANDSCAPE DESIGN: MYLES BALDWIN DESIGN
BUILDER: HORIZON

BRIDGEVIEW

A strong architectural envelope informed the approach
to the interiors of this striking home

'WE WERE STRONGLY INFLUENCED BY THESE CURVED SYDNEY SANDSTONE WALLS ... BUT THEIR DOMINATION REQUIRED A NUANCED APPROACH TO THE INTERIORS TO SOFTEN THE IMPACT OF THE RAW STONE.'

Sometimes what you can see doesn't tell the whole story! Our clients, who lived overseas and were planning to return to Sydney, were unable to view the property during the pandemic. They bought this four-storey house sight unseen, relying only on photos and real estate agents. After a closer inspection by friends and builders, it became clear that there were issues with the finishes of the house that required major remediation.

The team retained to work on the house felt a heightened sense of responsibility, as the owners were still overseas and all communication with them was online. Their initial brief, for a refined and detailed interior, expanded as the scope of the work required grew.

The architects for the original build were not retained after the design phase. The architectural intention was to celebrate Sydney Harbour's yachting narrative through curved walls that reference giant sails. We were strongly influenced by these curved Sydney sandstone walls, which are expressed from the exterior and flow into parts of the home, but their domination required a nuanced approach to the interiors to soften the impact of the raw stone. We selected a variety of timber veneers, including figured eucalyptus and ghost anegre, to punctuate the long entrance hall, soften the effect of the stone, conceal cupboards and subtly demarcate the lift and the guest cloakroom with bronze vertical columns.

In the kitchen, lighter bronze tones reflect the colour of the sandstone. The dark timber floor, laid in a chevron pattern, mitigates the light that floods the northern and western areas and anchors the soft tones of the marble that dominates the kitchen.

The north-eastern wing, located on the right as you enter the home, was reconfigured to create a study for our client. It connects to a small rumpus room and play area, making it ideal for working from home while keeping an eye on the kids. Directly above this wing, enveloped by curved sandstone and glass, we replanned the space to accommodate two bedrooms and a shared bathroom for the children.

Despite the distance, communication with the owners was excellent. They were decisive and responsive to our presentations, from concept to full construction documentation, and were clear about their preferences. When we felt strongly about a design issue, they were willing to take our advice on board. One such issue was the staircase that links all four levels and is prominent from the moment you open the front door. While the position of the staircase is unchanged, we replaced the clumsy glass balustrade with a finely curved sculptural one and highlighted it with cascading pendants. It has transformed this space.

Another space required a very creative solution. When the owners discovered that one of the downstairs bedrooms had ceilings that were 4.7 metres high, they saw an opportunity to use it as a fun space for their children and their friends. We rose to the challenge, creating what is essentially an elevated playground and bunk bedroom, that caters for overnight visitors. It is everything the owners imagined and the youngest members of the family love it.

We normally combine the interior design of our projects with the interior decoration. This home is an exception, as the owner selected most of the furniture from the United States with the assistance of an American interior decorator.

PREVIOUS: The large front door has a bronze inset and a handle made from Estivo marble, and pivots open to reveal a view through a frameless window.

OPPOSITE: Gun barrel view of the Sydney Harbour Bridge from the upstairs study.

ABOVE: View from the entry, with a sandstone wall on the right, through the living area to the outdoor terrace.

ABOVE: The new balustrade was carefully built around the existing staircase, above which a Lee Broom Chamber chandelier cascades in three tiers.

OPPOSITE: The overhead cupboards are clad in a warm metallic Axolotl finish.

ABOVE: The dark timber cladding in the background wraps around into the entry walkway, defining the kitchen. The island bench is wrapped in Silver Adana marble with an Apparatus Trapeze Mobile pendant overhead.

OPPOSITE: The informal dining table next to the kitchen, with glass-fronted, marble-lined cupboards behind.

OPPOSITE: The small room next to the owner's study is intended as a play or study area for the children. The Aceto rug, designed by Cristina Repeti, is from our collection.

ABOVE: In the guest cloakroom, a slab of Calacatta marble holds a Falper Eccentrico basin finished in Pietra Grey marble, with an elegant Gessi basin mixer in antique brass.

ABOVE: Details from the main bedroom, with a painting by Seaneen Tait above the console.

OPPOSITE: The neutral shades in the main bedroom are punctuated with an aubergine throw. The view from the bed is of Sydney Harbour and the north shore.

OPPOSITE: We designed the main ensuite vanity in keeping with the language of curves in the architecture.

ABOVE: Detail of the main dressing room.

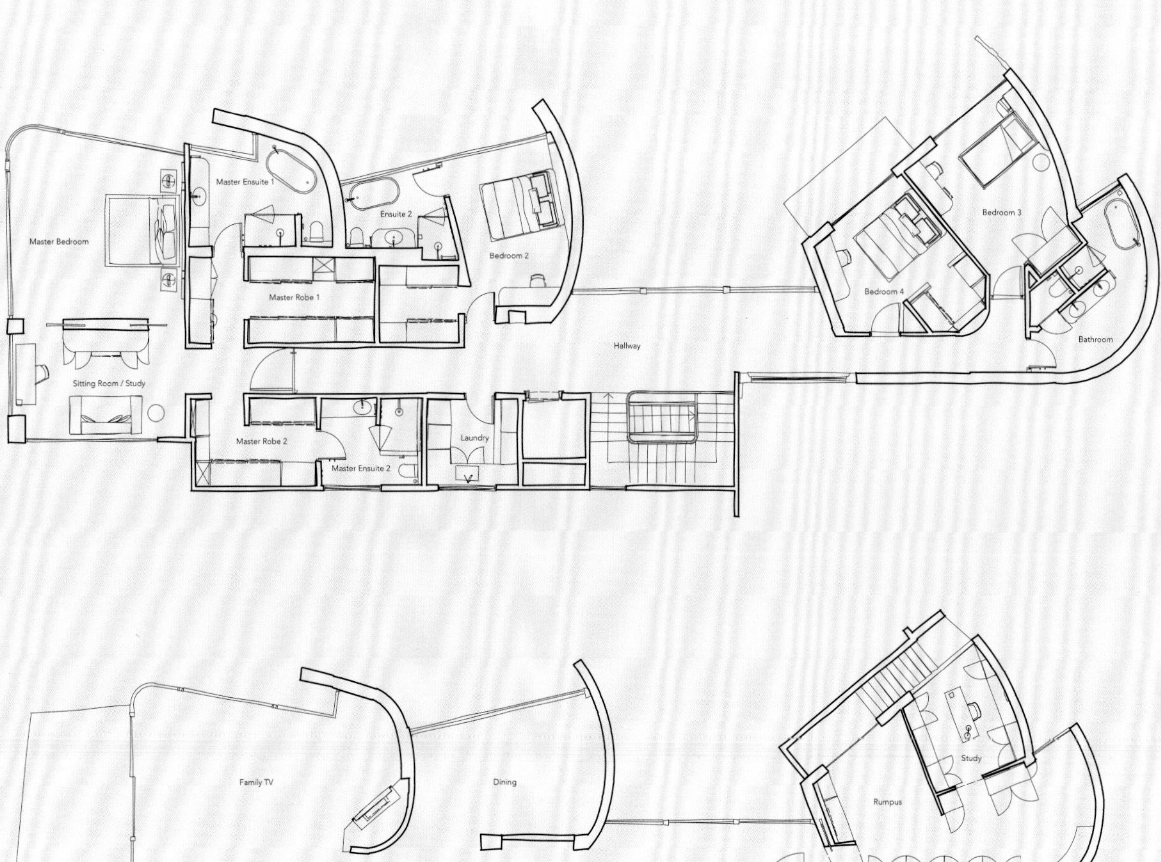

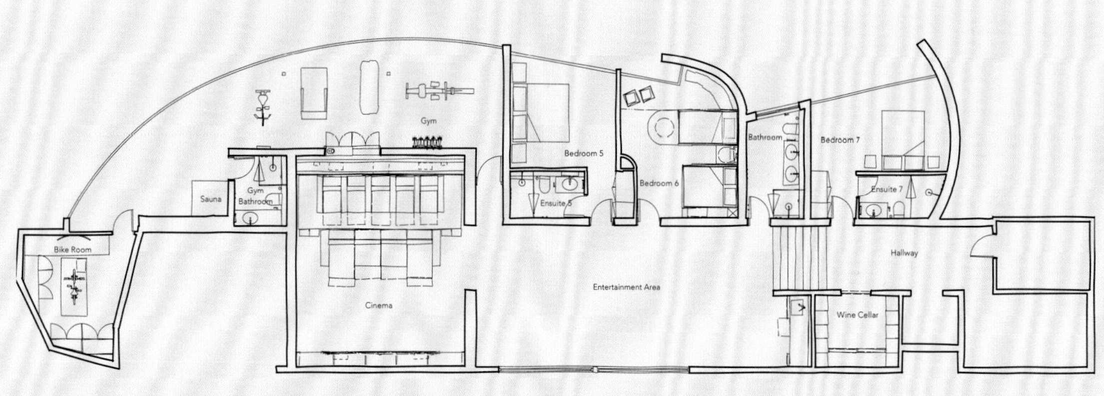

OPPOSITE: The main entry is flanked by a towering sandstone wall.

DESIGN INSIGHT: BUNK FUN

Repurposing a voluminous space into a playful bunk room

During the demolition of parts of the interior of Bridgeview, a large cavity was discovered in the ceiling of a downstairs bedroom, originally intended to house bunk beds. The room was intended for visiting children, but the owners quickly realised that it could be more than that. They asked us to design a triple-volume bunk/playroom.

Making good use of the ceiling height, we developed a plan to construct two levels of bunks, with a double and single bed on each level. This left enough room for a play area on top that could be accessed by a steep ladder. Another ladder links the second level to a strategically placed, softly upholstered seat, just in case someone decides to jump! There are also playful niches, shaped as portholes, that have built-in shelves and drawers for storage.

Through a consultant, we submitted the plans to the Australian Building Codes Board to ensure that they complied with the National Construction Code. We subsequently made some changes, a process that was important to ensure everyone's safety.

The room has been an absolute hit! Combining the elements of a cubby house with a playground has proved to be the key to entertaining children for hours.

DESIGNER: CRISTINA REPETI

MANUFACTURED BY: ENTH DEGREE PROJECTS

MATERIALS: PLYWOOD, CURVED PLYWOOD, OAK, POLYURETHANE, FABRIC

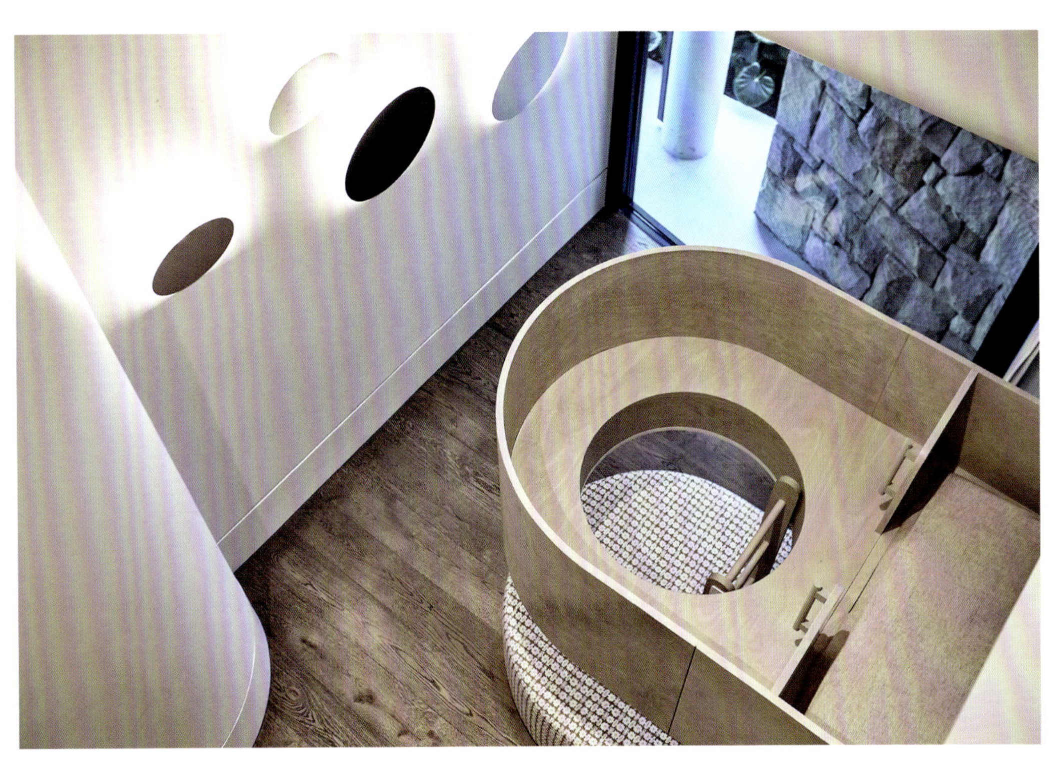

INTERIOR DESIGN: CRISTINA REPETI & MERYL HARE
INTERIOR DECORATION: MERYL HARE
ARCHITECTURE: CARLISLE ARCHITECTS

BEHIND THE PINES

Light, shadows and the surrounding colours of nature are reflected in the relaxed ambience of this coastal penthouse

'ON REFLECTION, SOME OF OUR COLOUR CHOICES WERE SUBLIMINAL, RATHER THAN LITERAL, MADE AS WE INSTINCTIVELY RESPONDED TO THE ENVIRONMENT.'

This penthouse overlooks North Steyne Beach in Manly, a beachside suburb in northern Sydney. Manly was named by Captain Arthur Phillip for the Indigenous Kay-ye-my people who lived here for thousands of years before Europeans arrived. Phillip stated that 'their confidence and manly behaviour made me give the name of Manly Cove to this place'. It is accessible from the centre of Sydney by road, but also has a ferry service that takes just thirty minutes from Circular Quay in the city. Manly was once advertised as 'seven miles from Sydney and a thousand miles from care'!

The owners were also the developers of the site. They engaged the architect to design three floors of apartments and their home, which takes up the top two floors of the building. It is positioned directly behind a row of Norfolk Island pines that were originally planted in the late 1800s. These trees are now an iconic feature of Manly. It is a beautiful position, taking in views of some of the best surfing beaches in Sydney.

The kitchen is the feature of the main living area, and we designed it with function, form and aesthetics front of mind. The colour of the feature marble reflects the sea, which is in full view from this room. We selected dark joinery to mitigate the strong natural light that dominates the space and articulated the curve of the architectural envelope on one side.

There is a relaxed ambience to this penthouse, which is in keeping with the owners' lifestyle and its proximity to the beach. In both the hard and soft finishes, we used colours that reflect the sea and surrounds. Soft grey concrete is the colour of the sea on a rainy day. Light, sand-coloured timber floors echo the beach. Blue like the water on a sunny day. Shades of white reference the white crests of the waves, and the charcoal is for the rocks and kelp. On reflection, some of our colour choices were subliminal, rather than literal, made as we instinctively responded to the environment.

Natural light plays a significant role in this interior, with windows and doors on all sides, as well as skylights. This creates shadows and bright contrasts, which we have taken advantage of in areas such as the powder room, where the bronze screen sends shadows across the room.

This penthouse feels like a freestanding home floating high above the lively bustle of the crowds below.

PREVIOUS: A collection of three totems by artist Ruth Levine stands on the plinth extension.

OPPOSITE: The curve of the southern wall is evident in the background of the kitchen cabinet. Ritzwell overlapping coffee tables in walnut in the foreground.

ABOVE: A Longwave armchair by Moroso in the intimate seating area off the main living room.

PREVIOUS: The Ocean Grey marble of the kitchen island and splashbacks is aptly named, and subtly reflects the ocean below. The dark timber veneer joinery creates a dramatic backdrop.

ABOVE: The appliance pantry is detailed in the same finishes as the rest of the kitchen.

OPPOSITE: The staircase walls are finished in a custom stucco applied by Hermosa Painting Finishes, and the treads and risers are Aren Bianco raw-sawn stone tiles.

OPPOSITE: The combined bath and shower in the wet area of the main ensuite features Statue Bronze tapware and walls finished in microcement.

ABOVE LEFT: The vanity in the main ensuite is a Grigio Imperiale marble trough with a Vixel glass mosaic splashback.

ABOVE RIGHT: Detail of a guest bathroom with handmade Spanish wall tiles.

ABOVE: Detail of a guest powder room vanity finished in Elegant Grey marble.

OPPOSITE: In this highly detailed room, the vanity joinery and screening poles are finished in bronze and an Apparatus Trapeze wall light is mounted next to the propped mirror.

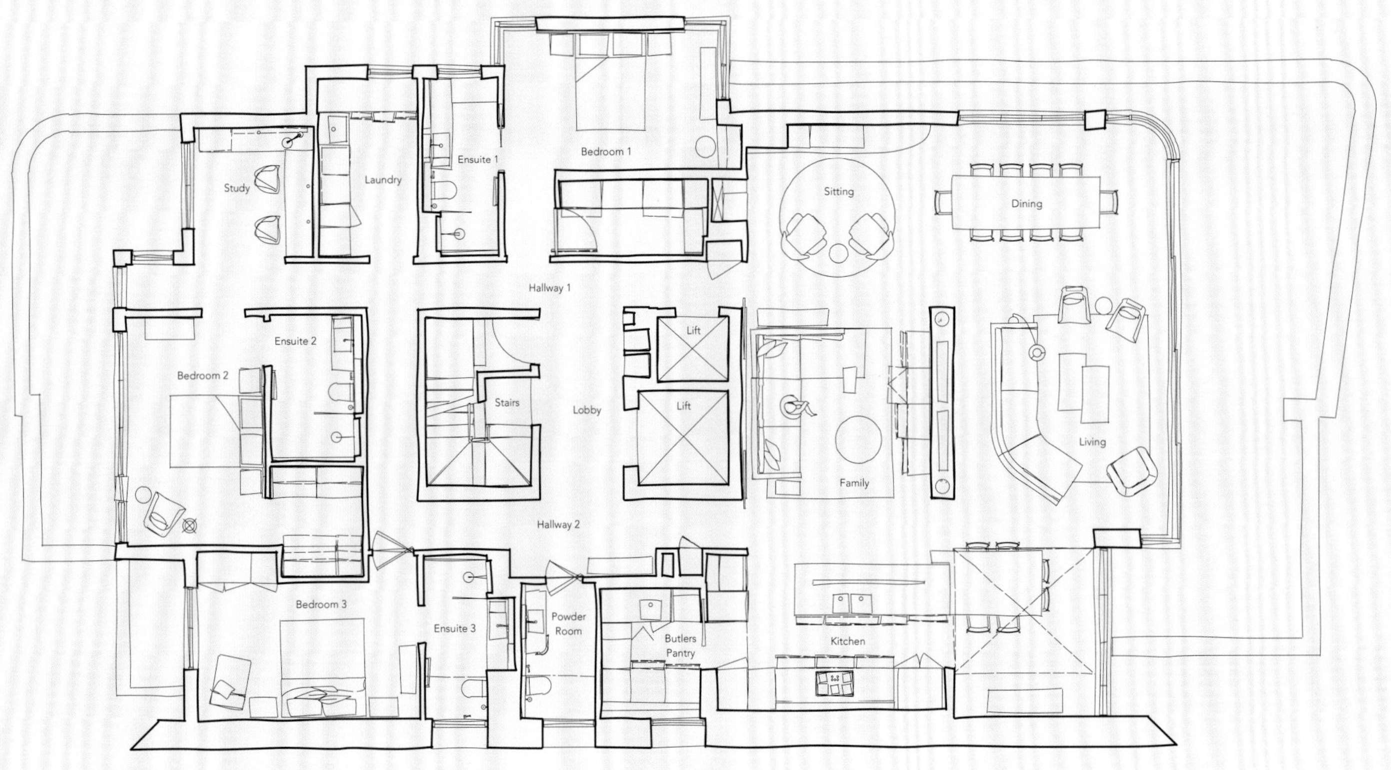

OPPOSITE: The view from the penthouse, directly towards the Pacific Ocean through the Norfolk Island Pine trees.

DESIGN INSIGHT: THE BANKS

A classic contemporary piece with a nod to Art Deco

The Banks was originally designed a few years ago as a double-sided room divider. In that instance the back and front appeared the same, although the drawers were only on one side. We have made it with or without a marble top and in different timber colours, depending on the interior we designed. There is a subtle nod to Art Deco in its design, but the Banks is essentially a classic contemporary piece, much like its namesake, my grandson!

It is a solid piece of furniture with a certain formality, particularly with the marble top; however, it is also defined by the objects that are placed on it. It was interesting looking back at our original concept sketch, as it hasn't really changed over the years that we've been making it, which is why I think it qualifies as a 'classic'.

The Banks is constructed in solid timber and has custom-made metal handles with a bronze finish. When made without a marble top, the base and drawers are in an open-grain finish, and the top has a deeper stain with a closed-grain finish. In Behind the Pines, it sits in the entry to the penthouse against a dark stucco wall.

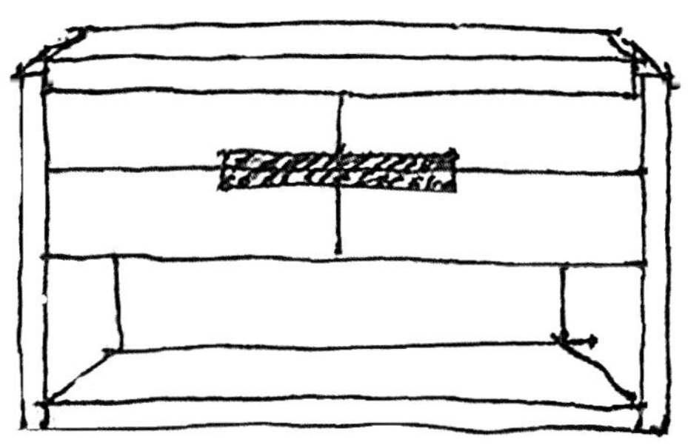

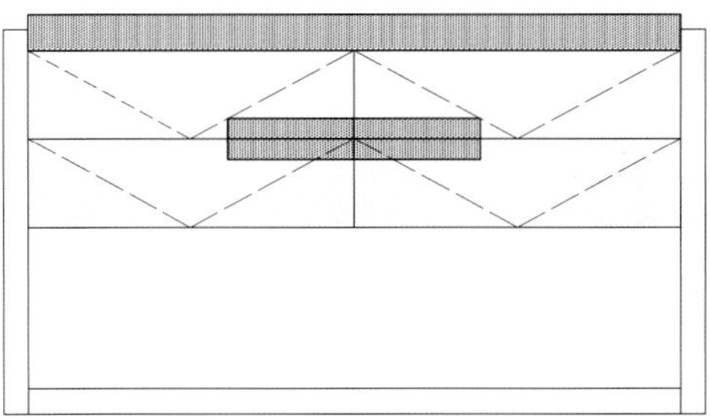

DESIGNER: HARE + KLEIN STUDIO

MANUFACTURED: SYDNEY

MATERIALS: OPEN-GRAIN-STAINED OAK, CLOSED-GRAIN-OAK OR MARBLE, BRONZE HANDLES

ARTWORK CREDITS

WOOLLAHRA TERRACE

14 Paintings on wall beside window by David Pearce (top) and Jenny Sages

16 Painting above mantle by Merryl Greaves; painting on right-hand shelf by Luke Sciberras

18 Painting by unknown artist; object on right-hand side of console by Ruth Levine

20–21 Painting on far wall by Joan Macy

22 Frame 1: Painting by Joe Furlonger

Frame 2: Paintings by David Pearce (top left), Tom Carment (top middle), Amanda Penrose Hart (bottom middle), David Pearce (top right), Joanna Logue (bottom left) and Amanda Penrose Hart (bottom right)

23 Paintings on left-hand shelf by Robyn Kinsela

24 Painting by Robyn Kinsela

25 Painting above mantel by Susie Dureau

28 Painting by David Pearce

THE CHATEAU

56 *The Wet* (2022) by Guido Maestri

57 Ceramics by Karlien van Rooyen (left, middle left and middle right) and Kerryn Levy (right)

58–59 Sculpture by Guido Maestri; *Head of the Table* (2020) by Ben Quilty

62 Sculpture by Cassie Thring; *NEO Shield (Near Earth Object)* (2013) by David Booth (Ghostpatrol)

63 *Red in Recline* (2000) by Deborah Paauwe

64–65 *Lantana Camara II* (porcelain) (2017) by Vipoo Srivilasa; sculpture by Paul Sloan; ceremonial pole by Garawan Wanambi; painting by William Mackinnon

66 *The Game is Up* by Sally Bourke

67 *The Future is Your Ocean Oyster* (2020) by Juz Kitson

68–69 *Supreme* by Fiona McMonagle

72 *Lattice* (2017–18) (left) and *Aurifera* (2020–21) (right) by Justine Varga

THE BEACH

78 Painting by Jenny Sages

81 Painting by Martin King

82 *Termite Mounds* by Elisabeth Cummings

84–85 *Time Shifted* by Jenny Sages (left); painting by Emily Kame Kngwarreye (right)

86 Watercolours by Joan Macy

88 *After the Fire* by Ildiko Kovacs (left); painting by Jenny Sages (right)

89 Ceramic bowl by Ruth Levine

90 Paintings by unknown artist from Santiago, Chile

91 Painting by Amanda Penrose Hart

94 Painting by Elisabeth Cummings

TAYLORS BAY

105 Painting by Beryl Miles

106 Ceramic totems by Ruth Levine

109 Paintings on shelves by Merryl Greaves

113 Painting by Joanna Kitas

SKYLINE PENTHOUSE

120 Painting by Sharon Candy

121 Painting by Joan B.N.V. Gent

122 Painting by unknown Hungarian artist

123 Paintings by unknown Hungarian artists

124 Ceramics by Ruth Levine and Laura Jankelson

125 Painting by Jo Davenport; sculpture by Valerie Andrianoff

128 Ceramic by Ruth Levine

129 Painting by Rosemary Valadon

131 Painting by Antony Bullimore

132 Painting by Elefteria Vlavianos

SADDLE HOUSE

136 Outdoor sculpture by David Ball; Larrakitj poles by Djirrirra Wunungmurra Yukuwa

140 Painting by Hannah van der Wal

141 Ceramic by Ruth Levine (bottom shelf)

142–143 Painting by Regina Pilawuk Wilson

148 Artwork by Gaypalani Wanambi

PEPPERMINT GROVE

158 Painting by Ian de Souza

160–161 Paintings by John Olsen (left) and Marise Maas (right)

162 Paintings by Marise Maas (left) and Arthur Boyd (right)

163 Artwork by NyapaNyapa

164 Painting by Arthur Boyd

165 Frame 1: Artwork by NyapaNyapa

Frame 2: Painting by Marise Maas

167 Painting by Judith White

168–169 Painting by Judith White

170 Painting by Joie Villeneuve

174 Painting by John Olsen

175 Totems by Ruth Levine; painting by Pierre-Auguste Renoir

OCEAN FRONT

184 Painting by James Drinkwater

192–193 Painting by Sharon Candy

197 Painting by Merryl Greaves

MANDEMAR

202 Painting by Ewoud de Groot

206–207 Painting by Luke Sciberras

208 Paintings by Charmaine Pwerle

209 Painting by Pierre-Marie Brisson

210–211 Painting by Charmaine Pwerle

217 Paintings by Stephanie Brancatisano (left) and Catherine Sim (centre)

HARBOURSIDE RESIDENCE

222 Sculpture by Jim Flook

226 Painting by Sophie Cape

232 Painting by John Wolseley

EDGE HOUSE

242 Mirror artwork by Ettore Sottsass

244 Ceramic by Ruth Levine

245 Painting by Kerry Armstrong

246–247 Wall sculpture by Dion Horstmans

259 Painting by Jo Bertini

BRIDGEVIEW

272 Painting by Seaneen Tait

275 Ceramic by Ruth Levine

BEHIND THE PINES

282 Ceramics by Ruth Levine

285 Ceramic by Ruth Levine (right middle)

ACKNOWLEDGEMENTS

300 Painting by Karl Martens

ACKNOWLEDGEMENTS

This is the third book that I have been privileged to work on with Paulina de Laveaux. She has guided me with her gentle but incisive manner, and I thank her for her enormous contribution. Daniel New has designed both this and my last book. He brings his special talents to making the content look better than I could have ever imagined, for which I thank him. To Lorna Hendry, who corrected my dubious grammar, Rachel Carter, Amanda Louey and Team Thames & Hudson – I have enjoyed working with you; thank you for your time and patience.

This book would not be possible without the talent and creativity of our amazing Hare + Klein Team – both past and present. Their contribution is at the core of this book. Every working day that I spend with them is a joy and I salute their integrity and work ethic. I hope that this book captures the essence of their projects so that, come what may, they are more than memories, and that they can reflect with pride on the work that they have achieved. Special thanks to Cristina, Kristie, Maddie, Bianca and Mel for your help with this book.

To our talented photographer, Jen Wilding, who is responsible for most of the images, I thank you. We have enjoyed working together for many years, and you've approached your role as designer with the same ability to perceive and capture beauty.

We couldn't do what we love doing without our clients, with whom we travel together on creative journeys, sometimes over several years. They put their trust in us to create homes that enrich their lives, giving joy and comfort.

The architects, builders, landscape designers, joiners, upholsterers, suppliers and artisans with whom we have forged partnerships with over many years, we couldn't do any of this without you. We are enormously grateful.

And we thank the partners and families of our team for their support, especially when we are caught up in deadlines and forget the time! This book is a celebration of the collective legacy of all the above collaborators, you know who you are!

BY THE LIGHT OF THE SEA

ABOUT HARE + KLEIN

Meryl Hare OAM is the Principal of Hare + Klein, formed in 1990. She is a Fellow of the Design Institute of Australia and has received a DIA citation for services to the design industry. She was inducted into the DIA Hall of Fame in 2011, and subsequently into the House and Garden Hall of Fame in 2018 and the Belle Hall of Fame in 2021. In 2020 she was awarded the IDEA Gold Medal Award and nominated as a Luminary at the 2022 INDE Awards. In 2024 she was awarded the Medal of the Order of Australia for her contribution to design.

The philosophy of the practice is embedded in enriching lives through design. This philosophy is reflected in Hare + Klein's own work, in their design choices and in the partners that they collaborate with. It is their strong conviction that an interior should balance aesthetics with layers of visual generosity.

The experienced and highly regarded studio of award-winning interior designers are committed to responding to their clients' brief and lifestyle, creating original, authentic interiors that stand the test of time.

Hare + Klein are five-time winners of the Australian Interior Design Awards, among many other awards. The practice has also been selected for the prestigious Andrew Martin International Design Review, appearing in fifteen volumes. This is the third book that Meryl has authored, published by Thames & Hudson.

First published in Australia in 2026 by Thames & Hudson Australia
Wurundjeri Country, 132A Gwynne Street, Cremorne, Victoria 3121

First published in the United Kingdom in 2026 by Thames & Hudson Ltd
6–24 Britannia Street, London WC1X 9JD

29 28 27 26 5 4 3 2 1

ISBN 978-1-760-76538-5

EU Authorized Representative: Interart S.A.R.L.
19 rue Charles Auray, 93500 Pantin, Paris, France
productsafety@thameshudson.co.uk
www.interart.fr

A catalogue record for this book is available from the National Library of Australia

A CIP catalogue record for this book is available from the British Library

Front cover: Peppermint Grove
Back cover: Saddle House
Photographer: Jen Wilding

Design: Daniel New
Editing: Lorna Hendry
Printed and bound in China by C&C Offset Printing Co., Ltd

Thames & Hudson Australia wishes to acknowledge that Aboriginal and Torres Strait Islander peoples are the first storytellers of this nation and the Traditional Custodians of the land on which we live and work. We acknowledge their continuing culture and pay respect to Elders past and present.
thamesandhudson.com.au